An Unexpected Journal

Courage, Strength, & Hope

Fall 2018

Volume 1, Issue 3

CONTENTS

REASON FOR OUR HOPE: THE ROLE OF FAIRY STORIES IN CHRISTIAN APOLOGETICS

Nicole Howe on Why Fairy Stories Matter

One of the objectives of Christian apologetics is to heed Peter's instruction to "always be prepared to give an answer to everyone who asks you to give the reason for the hope that you have."[1] Much attention is often placed on the word "reason," bringing to mind ideas of philosophical arguments, logical explanations, and scientific claims. Thus, we might walk away from Peter's instruction assuming our primary duty is to build a case for the existence of Christ based on factual evidence alone. After all, the word "apologetics" comes from the word "apologia," which means "defense." This word

---

[1] 1 Pet 3:15

easily stirs up images of a courtroom and the stern face of a judge whose primary role is to deliver a verdict based on a presentation of facts.

However, in our effort to build a case for Christianity, we should not forget that what we are trying to communicate – what is really on trial here – is our *hope.* And the hope that is in each one of us involves an Event so enormous and mysterious it can scarcely be put into words. Communicating the historical evidence for the resurrection of Christ is important, but equally important is communicating why this evidence matters. The case we are making in this courtroom involves the greatest story ever told – a story of a God who lived as one of us, died as one of us, and rose again to make us like Himself. It is a story of courage, heroism, suffering, deliverance, death, resurrection, and final victory – a "true myth,"[2] as Lewis called it. We have much to learn from great thinkers such as Lewis, MacDonald, Chesterton, and Tolkien who knew how to harness the power of story in order to effectively communicate the truth, goodness, and beauty of the Christian faith. Bare facts are not enough; we must give these facts meaning.

---

[2] C S. Lewis, *The Collected Letters of C.S. Lewis* (San Francisco: HarperSanFrancisco, 2004), 977.

Enter literary apologetics – the branch of apologetics that utilizes the power of story to communicate the Christian faith. The entire concept of literary apologetics can be a stumbling block for some, as the word itself can seem a bit oxymoronic. While the word "literary" points to the realm of the imagination, the word "apologetics" points to the realm of reason and evidence. This can trip us up, because in our post-Enlightenment era, we have (often subconsciously) bought into the idea that reason and imagination are two separate faculties that oppose one another. In his essay, "The Imagination: Its Function and its Culture," George MacDonald describes the prevailing opinion that a high regard for the imagination supposedly results in a rejection of facts and what can be known for the acceptance of fancies and mere inventions.[3] This false dichotomy has been the source of many ills, perhaps none as apparent as the assumed rift between science and religion. Too often, we regard the imagination as "the one faculty before all others to be suppressed,"[4] and even well-meaning Christians have fallen into this trap. MacDonald

---

[3]. George MacDonald, *The Imagination: Its Function and its Culture*, accessed Sept. 9, 2016, http://www.george-macdonald.com/etexts/the_imagination.html.

[4] Ibid.

opposes this idea, claiming that the imagination is itself an important region for discovery.[5] Therefore, if we hope to properly understand the value of literary apologetics, we must first settle the issue on the value of the imagination and how it relates to reason.

The power of the imagination to absorb information is well demonstrated by the fact that many Christians have accepted the false dichotomy between reason and imagination without actually knowing from whence it came. As MacDonald asserts, "it is not the things we see the most clearly that influence us the most powerfully."[6] The imagination is not simply a faculty existing for the purpose of creating mere fancies or imaginary worlds, it is the foundation in which we begin our quest for reality and truth. It "gives form to thought,"[7] MacDonald says. Many times the influence of the imagination is hidden and unnoticed, but whether or not we recognize its power, even science cannot get out from under it. MacDonald tells us that "a prudent question is half

---

[5] Ibid.

[6] Ibid.

[7] Ibid.

the knowledge"[8] Before the scientist goes about testing that which the eye can see, there is the "scaffolding of hypothesis," the often unnoticed glimmer in his eye, without which the "house of science could never arise."[9] Or put another way, "the intellect must labour, workman-like under the direction of the architect, Imagination."[10] We should begin to see that to separate reason and imagination is all but impossible, for reason cannot exist without the imagination.

A correct understanding of the interdependence between reason and imagination sheds new light on the benefit of literary apologetics. Many people are unable to accept philosophical or reasoned arguments for Christianity until their minds have been supplied with foundational ideas that can give these arguments meaning. While "science may pull the snowdrop to shreds," it "cannot find out the idea of suffering hope and pale confident submission."[11] At the same time, we may absolutely exhaust ourselves providing historical evidence for the resurrection of Christ, never

---

[8] Ibid.

[9] Ibid.

[10] Ibid.

[11] Ibid.

realizing that these arguments are devoid of meaning to someone whose imagination has not first been engaged. Truth does not really exist until it *means* something. Lewis, Tolkien, MacDonald, and Chesterton all recognized that igniting the imagination allows us to communicate truth in a way that is deeply meaningful, engaging the person's mind, heart, and soul. By interacting with others through stories, we invite them to slow down and experience the truths of God's word. Ideas like redemption, honor, heroism, good, and evil are better understood when we can think, feel, and imagine how they play out in a created world. Fairy stories then, are not just for children.

The attempt to define the essence of a fairy story is challenging, and even Tolkien admits in *On Fairy Stories* that it cannot be caught "in a net of words."[12] Fairy stories do not depend on the "historical account of an elf or fairy," but upon "the nature of Faerie: The Perilous Realm itself, and the air that blows in that country."[13] The nearest Tolkien can come to this idea with words is to offer us "Magic."[14] The first thing we must leave behind

---

[12] Tolkien, J.R.R., *On Fairy-stories* (London: HarperCollins, 2014), 32.

[13] Ibid.

[14] Ibid.

is the assumption that the magic of Faerie is only for children, for Tolkien tells us that "if a fairy-story as a kind is worth reading at all it is worthy to be written for and read by adults."[15] While many of us are tempted to assume that adulthood brings with it a maturity unfit for Faerie, Lewis asks, "who in his senses would not keep, if he could, that tireless curiosity, that intensity of imagination, that facility of suspending disbelief, that unspoiled appetite, that readiness to wonder, to pity, and to admire?"[16] We should hope to hang onto this keen ability for the "process of growing up is to be valued for what we gain, not for what we lose."[17]

The reason we must never outgrow our appreciation for fairy stories is because the story of God coming to earth, dying, and rising again could not be considered anything less than magical, should we discover it in the pages of a fairy tale. The hope of the Gospel message does not lie in a compilation of facts; rather it is a work of art, crafted by a creative God. Our very lives are a part of that story – a part of God's magnum opus. The

---

[15] Ibid, 58.

[16] C.S. Lewis, *An Experiment in Criticism* (London: Cambridge University Press, 1961), 72.

[17] Ibid.

Bible tells us that we are God's "poiema," His masterpiece.[18] It makes sense then that we might better understand the meaning of our lives through works of art rather than philosophical arguments. God's creation, including both man and Nature, points to the glory of God through its beauty. It inspires awe and wonder, connecting us more easily to feelings of gratitude and worship. In the same way God has communicated His glory through His creation, we can communicate through our own "sub-creations."[19] We ourselves write stories that elicit awe and wonder, because it is in His wisdom that "we move and live and have our being."[20] Fairy stories reflect God's character, not just through their magical plots and other-world adventures, but also by the very act of their creation.

Not only do fairy stories mirror the magical quality of the Gospel story, as well as point to the idea of a Creative God who is the author of world, even the reading of a fairy story can prepare us to rightly receive truth, as Lewis explains in *An Experiment in Criticism*. This suggests that there is a

---

[18] Eph 2:10.

[19] Tolkien, *On Fairy Stories*, 59.

[20] MacDonald, *The Imagination: Its Function and its Culture*.

correct way to read a fairy story. Sadly, because fairy stories have too often been "relegated to the nursery as shabby or old-fashioned furniture is relegated to the play-room,"[21] many of us have lost the ability to read fairy stories well, if not for anything but a lack of practice. Our post-Enlightenment mindset might be a contributor to this underserved banishment, as Lewis describes the unliterary as having the kind of limited vision and narrowed focus that is not unlike what we discover when we isolate reason from imagination. If the rational person wants only the facts and no meaning, so the "unliterary reader wants only the Event." He "ignores nearly all that the words before him are doing; he wants to know what happened next."[22] This is what Lewis refers to as "using" a story. We seek to get out of it what we want, discarding the rest like a "burnt-out match."[23]

In comparison, a literary person is one who surrenders to the work of art, willing to "receive" the story in its totality, appreciating it for the thing that it is rather than what it might do for him in the

---

[21] Tolkien, *On Fairy Stories*, 50.

[22] Lewis, *An Experiment in Criticism*, 30.

[23] Ibid., 2.

moment.[24] Unlike the cold rationalism of the user, the receiver does not dismantle a work of art for the bits and pieces he can conquer and therefore put to use; rather, he allows the work to overtake him, surrendering himself to the journey of discovery and adventure, wherever the road may lead. Lewis emphasizes that "the first demand any work of any art makes upon us is surrender. Look. Listen. Receive. Get yourself out of the way."[25] One could hardly read these words and not recognize the bridge Lewis builds between our ability to receive a fairy-story and our ability to receive the Gospel story. Surrender, vulnerability, and receptiveness are much needed ingredients to appreciate magic of any sort, including that which lies in the mystery of the Gospel. Is it any wonder we are told in Scripture that we must have a heart of a child to receive the kingdom? Let us never relegate humility, surrender, and patient wonder to the nursery. For we serve a God who "took delight to hide his works, to the end to have them found out; as if kings could not obtain a greater honour than to be God's playfellows in that game."[26]

---

[24] Ibid., 19.

[25] Ibid., 19.

[26] MacDonald, *The Imagination: Its Function and its Culture.*

We would do well to acknowledge that this "game" is so often only half-apprehended by the mind of a skeptic and can present itself to the doubting man as a sinister game of cat and mouse, whereas we are not so much God's playfellows as we are His playthings. The problem of evil and human suffering is perhaps one of the most significant stumbling blocks to the rationalist and poet alike and is quite often a preventative to the kind of humility and surrender needed for full receptivity of the Gospel. Fairy stories can work well to prepare the imagination and assist in the mind's ability to conceive not only of dryads but also of orcs.

To a skeptic's mind, the idea of a good God who is all-powerful creating a world consisting of both the beautiful as well as the ugly, is a "mathematical impossibility."[27] It simply does not add up. The existence of suffering and evil in our world has been a source of great angst since it was birthed in the Garden of Eden. In fact, Tolkien explains that many fairy stories have appeared throughout the history of mankind for the very reason that they provide an Escape from "hunger, thirst, poverty,

---

[27] G.K. Chesterton, "The Ethics of Elfland" from *Orthodoxy*, accessed Sept. 9, 2016, http://www.ccel.org/ccel/chesterton/orthodoxy.vii.html.

pain, sorrow, injustice, and death."[28] The "Consolation of the Happy Ending" speaks to "the oldest and deepest desire - the Escape from Death."[29] This kind of escape should not be confused with mere escapism, to be equated with the "flight of the deserter,"[30] It is more noble than that, similar to a man who finds himself in prison and longs to break free.[31]

What fairy stories offer us then is the chance to experience a world where magic, beauty and goodness indeed exist alongside evil – both rationally and imaginatively. In fact, a fairy story would not be a fairy story without orcs, trolls, and evil men. What shall the hero fight against? What would courage look like in the absence of danger? Should we ever hope to understand such concepts of health, vitality, and justice if not for the existence of their counterpart? Through fairy stories, we can see that it is logically coherent for beauty and evil to co-exist without evil having the final say. With all its imaginative undertakings, fairy stories still exhibit order, what Tolkien calls,

---

[28] Tolkien, *On Fairy Stories*, 73.

[29] Ibid., 74 - 75.

[30] Ibid., 69

[31] Ibid.

"an inner consistency of reality."[32] It is for this reason Chesterton reveals in *Orthodoxy* that fairy tales always seemed to him to be "entirely reasonable things."[33] For while they are filled with "bodily miracles," they never contain "mathematical impossibilities."[34] We will never be able to conceive of one and two making anything other than three, neither in our world nor in Faerie.[35] But we should be surprised at how much we are able to accept. This inner consistency of reality disarms us just enough to separate the truly impossible from what is merely difficult to imagine. But for a moment, we find ourselves believing in happy endings, even in the presence of evil.

This Consolation of a Happy Ending is what Tolkien asserts all "complete fairy stories must have."[36] The name he gives to this is "Eucatastrophe." It is a "sudden, joyous turn . . . a miraculous grace: never to be counted on to

---

[32] Ibid., 60.

[33] Chesterton, *Orthodoxy*.

[34] Ibid.

[35] Ibid.

[36] Tolkien, *On Fairy Stories*, 75.

recur."[37] We see through the fairy story that no amount of opposition can hold back the tide from turning. The Happy Ending is always delivered. Eucatastrophe "denies (in the face of much evidence if you will) universal and final defeat and in so far is evangelium, giving a fleeting glimpse of Joy, Joy beyond the walls of the world, poignant as grief."[38] Where else but in fairy tale can we "try on" this idea and see that it can be rationally embraced? To whisper under hopeful breath, "oh death where is thy sting?"[39] It is the cynic who claims stories such as these arise if only to escape. It is the hope rising up in those on the precipice of belief which dares to suggest that they arise out of the deeper Truth that our world is not unlike a fairy tale and that, "however wild its events, however fantastic or terrible the adventures, it can give to child or man that hears it, when the 'turn' comes, a catch of the breath, a beat and lifting of the heart, near to (or indeed accompanied by) tears, as keen as that given by any form of literary art and having a peculiar quality."[40]

---

[37] Ibid.

[38] Ibid.

[39] 1 Cor 15:55.

[40] Ibid., 76.

This is perhaps the greatest value of fairy stories: to awaken the imagination and invite the reader to dare to believe that the lines between reason and imagination, science and religion, and even the Real World and Faerie lands are not as distinct as we think. Indeed, we see such stark division because we have lost the element of wonder in our own world. The sun still blazes on, yet we refuse to be dazzled. Cold rationality has chilled our fingers to the bone, making wonder impossible to grasp. Instead of marveling at the birth of a new life, we seek too often to destroy it. But wonder is "not a mere fancy derived from the fairy tales."[41] Chesterton reminds us that "all the fire of the fairy tales is derived from [wonder]. Just as we all like love tales because there is an instinct of sex, we all like astonishing tales because they touch the nerve of the ancient instinct of astonishment."[42] Our world is just as fantastic as any fairy tale, but we have "forgotten what we really are."[43] And even more, "all that we call common sense and rationality and practicality and

---

[41] Chesterton, *Orthodoxy*.

[42] Ibid.

[43] Ibid.

positivism only means that for certain dead levels of our life we forget that we have forgotten."[44]

Fairy stories help us to remember. They point back to the beauty and magic and wonder that exists in our own world. They tell us "apples were golden only to refresh the forgotten moment when we found that they were green. They make rivers run with wine only to make us remember, for one wild moment, that they run with water." [45] Is the magic of a hummingbird any less than the magic of a pixie?

In Peter's admonition, he also tells Christians to give our answer with gentleness and respect. This means we must always respect the person we are speaking to but also the Person we are speaking about. Let us remember that the "Gospels contain a fairy-story, or a story of a larger kind which embraces all the essence of fairy stories."[46] God used a story to communicate truth to us. Why should we do otherwise? The reason for our hope is wrapped up in the greatest story ever told. And like any good fairy tale, ours contains within it "the greatest and most complete conceivable

---

[44] Ibid.

[45] Ibid.

[46] Tolkien, 78.

eucatastrophe,"[47] a miraculous, grace-filled turn of events in which Christ escaped death once and for all of us. The miracle is that this event truly happened - it is a true story born out of the Imagination of God. And our Creator "is the Lord, of angels, and of men – and of elves. Art has been verified."[48] May we remember to keep the fantastic close by when we give a reason for our hope. There is no clear line between our world and Faerie, for "Legend and History have met and fused."[49]

Can there be anything more magical than that?

---

[47] Ibid.

[48] Ibid.

[49] Ibid.

THE ADVENTURES OF ASHER SVENSON: STORY ONE: THE SECRET WOOD

Lucas W. Holt on the Mystery of the Forest

A young man, a rugged youth,
Sought to find the truth
Of a mysterious wood –
In the midst of which he stood.

He talked with creatures that lived therein
To see if he could then begin
To find out just where he had come,
For all he knew was that he was far from home.

But for all the strangeness of the place,
One could see a change upon his face,
From dark and grave and full of fear
To light and grins and merry cheer.

Just what was in this wood, you ask?
Ah, now we have reached our task.
And so we begin to embark upon
The adventures of Asher Svenson.

There is a small, dense wood that lays hidden in the slopes of southern Oregon. Asher Svenson chanced to find it one morning on one of his Sunday long runs. How he had gotten to it was a mystery, but it was a place he would never forget. Within the wood are large, towering trees that stand like ancient pillars, which seem to stretch to the clouds and connect the earth to the heavens. Not only are the trees tall, but they possess a majestic quality, with their auburn colored bark and olive green leaves. When the sun breaks forth, a dome of dark green and gold covers the wood and dresses the mighty firs in robes of light. An aroma of cedar fills the air, tinged with scents of evergreen. The sound of birds calling back and forth to one another can be heard throughout the day. Towards the western side of the wood runs an ice blue stream that contrasts with a muddy, green embankment so strikingly that Asher once fancied he had stepped into a Monet painting. California poppy wildflowers dot the little clearings throughout the wood. When the sky darkens and the sun begins to set, the yellow-orange color of the wildflowers stand out like candles at compline.

Asher often called the secret wood "Elf Land," for he fancied that millions of years ago the wood was inhabited by elves. One day he decided to go on a walkabout to tour the wood to see if anything had changed since his last visit four months ago before he left for college. As he was walking, a strong wind came howling by that caused the leaves on the trees to rumble. The rumbling had a strange sound. It was as if it were not a rumbling but rather a snickering; like the wind had just given the punch line of a joke and the trees were in laughter. Asher began to feel that he was in a very different place than the small wood he once knew.

As Asher continued to walk through the wood he noticed what looked like a very odd tree. It had a large, dark hole in its trunk. Looking at it made him feel like he was staring into the mouth of a toothless giant. All of a sudden he could start to feel his heart thud against his chest. He looked up and down the tree, with its peeling bark, its bulging roots, and its branches stretching forth like the arms of an octopus. Then in a flash an owl came flying out of the dark hole, startling the young man so much that he actually fell back and began to breathe heavily. The owl alighted on a branch just to the right of where he lay and stared at him. Its eyes were gigantic, colored with a mix of gray and yellow, as if God had created two secret moons and hidden them on this owl's face: simply looking at its eyes could make one feel like they had grown in wisdom and intelligence. The young man started to tremble. He felt weak. His legs were like jelly, and he was unsure if he would be able to stand back up. What was the owl going to say? Was it going to say anything or just stare at him? Unsure of what to do, he quickly composed himself and gave a bow to the venerable owl. "And to what do I owe the pleasure of this visit?" he asked, with slight trepidation.

The owl said nothing. It just sat there and stared. Two minutes of silence ensued, which to Asher felt like an eternity. Then the owl finally replied, speaking in a soft voice with a slow cadence, "I had heard that there was a fellow roaming the wood and thought I'd come sit on a branch to see if I could chance upon a view of the lad. And here you are."

Surprised, Asher began to ask questions: "How did you hear of me? Where did you come from? Is that your home in there?" his eyes shifting toward the black hole.

"Well," responded the Owl, "it is a small wood, as you know, and news often travels with great rapidity. It did not take long for me to hear of a young man roaming about. The two sparrows who live near the river bend were eager to tell me about your arrival."

"Ah, interesting," replied Asher passively, being most interested in the last question. He reiterated, "But where did you come from? Is that hole in the trunk of the tree your home?"

"I think the more interesting question," replied the Owl, "is where did *you* come from? Surely your being here is more curious than me being here, wouldn't you agree?" With sinking heart and furrowed brow, Asher conceded that this was indeed true.

There was a moment's pause before the Owl asked, "What are you thinking about?"

"Well, Madame Owl, to be honest, I've been thinking about how this wood seems so strange. It is very different than what I remember." And then he said quietly to himself, half-jokingly but also half serious, "It's like the world at present". The Owl heard what the young man said, for she had very great ears.

She responded thoughtfully, "Ah, I see. You know, I believe that there is a purpose for your being here in this wood right now. It may seem strange, but I am of the opinion that strange things can be better indicators of what is true than what is regular. And yet, even seemingly normal things are strange, really. Why is the sky blue and not purple? Why is grass green and not red? But now I merely muse. Press on and keep exploring!"

Asher was a bit puzzled at her response but before he could form a coherent thought the Owl flew off. "What a curious creature!" he thought to himself. "I wonder if there are others in this wood as interesting as her." So he continued to walk throughout the wood, and as he did so he contemplated what the curious winged creature had said.

Pressing onward through the woods, another very peculiar tree caught the corner of his eye. It was visibly different from the others. Its branches reminded him of the antlers he saw on deer when he would go hunting with his grandfather as a boy. The branches emerged in every direction out of its trunk, one on top of the other. Not only did the branches look like antlers, but also they had the similar effect: a betrayal of distinction and importance. The trunk of the tree looked so firm and ancient that he thought it must have been there for thousands of years. Indeed, it had a sense of antiquity; but it also seemed new and fresh, like it had the ability to detach from its roots and leap to and fro with great finesse like a young fawn. Sparked with an immediate sense of curiosity the young man steadily approached it in great awe and wonder.

As he was approaching the tree it started to shake violently and the earth beneath him began quaking. It was as if the tree had been dead but upon Asher's arrival it came to life. Two giant pieces of bark began to fall from the center of its trunk, but it was not peeling bark: it was the tree opening its eyes. Then the tree started speaking, but it was the strangest thing because it had no visible mouth, only its voice could be heard. It sounded to Asher as if the voice were coming from inside the trunk. And had there been a large hole in the tree like the one the Owl flew out of, he was certain the volume of the tree's voice would have increased significantly and perhaps shattered to pieces the surrounding trees. It was such a lovely voice, though, and it sounded as if the tree was singing.

"What are you singing?" asked Asher in a moment of bravery.

"It is part of an old song that has been sung by many of the trees in this wood for a long time," said the Tree. "Would you like to hear it?"

"Yes, absolutely," said Asher.

For all our life we have lived under the sky,
Beholding the bright stars that shine above,
And indeed the moon and sun.
But of all the lights that ever were, none prove
Greater than the one that lingers close by.

O fair radiance! O shining brilliance!
Bright yellow, orange and red,
Thy light is like a flaming torch:
Which gives some delight and others dread,
But for us trees makes us want to dance!

"I quite like that!" exclaimed Asher.

"If only you heard the whole thing!" replied the Tree. "But, of course, that would probably take an hour or so. The song is really part of an old tale that tells the story of one of our ancient relatives named Roshanuk who was felled in a forest far away.

Anyhow, what brings a young man like you into this wood?"

"I've been trying to figure that out myself," said Asher. "In fact, I was just speaking with this owl not long ago who said"

"Oh! Mrs. Feathergloss!"

"Yes, Mrs. Feathergloss," said Asher slowly and curiously. "You know her, then?"

"Indeed I do. She is very kind, and incredibly wise. I often let her and her little ones come and perch on my branches."

"Ah, I see," said the young man.

The Tree fixed his eyes on the young man and asked, "What is your name?"

"Asher," the young man responded.

"Asher. That is a fine name. Let me ask you, Asher. Do you enjoy looking up at the stars at night?"

"I do," he said.

"So do I," said the Tree. "Would you like to know why?"

"I would," said Asher.

The Tree began, "Have you ever noticed how it is never completely dark? The sun governs the day, and the moon and the stars govern the night. There are always lights on. Looking up at the stars gives me hope. It reminds me that no matter how dark things may get, there is always hope. There's always a light shining in the darkness. Even on cloudy days the sun shines though we cannot see it."

"I had never really thought of it that way before. It is a rather comforting thought. And it is true." There was moment of silence between them, and then Asher asked, "But what is this other light that you sang about?"

"Ah, yes," the Tree replied. Then, taking a leafy limb and swinging it down near Asher, much like one stretches out an arm to place a hand on a shoulder, he said, "You will find it if you keep searching. Take courage, and continue on your quest, young friend!"

And with that the Tree shook violently just like it did when Asher first arrived, and then returned to its original state. Asher was sad that the conversation was over. He thoroughly enjoyed talking with the magnificently truncated tree. Then as he was getting ready to turn and walk away, a shiny object caught the corner of his eye. It was a small capsule lying at the bottom of the Tree's trunk. He walked over to it, and on the capsule was written the words: "Strength for the journey. Enjoy." Asher opened the top of the capsule and looked inside then took a whiff to see if he could tell what it was. It smelled sweet like syrup. Then he lifted it to his lips and threw his head back and drank a small portion of it. "Ah!" he exclaimed, "it is syrup!" The syrup was a rich, dark brown and tasted as sweet as it smelled. "What a great gift!" said the young man. And he stretched out his hand and placed it on the Tree's trunk looking at it with affection. He smiled and then continued walking.

What a day the young lad was having! He couldn't wait to tell his friend Miguel about all that had happened so far. He was so full of joy, basking in all that had occurred. His conversations with Mrs. Feathergloss and the Tree were incredible, and he was also enjoying the spectacular scenes of the wood in which he found himself. A feeling of joy began to well up inside of him to the point where it became hard to contain his emotions. He soon burst forth and began to dance, jumping into the air and shouting aloud.

Soon after, he decided to keep exploring. He was walking through the wood admiring its verdure. Everything was teeming with life. The branches of the tall trees were leafy and green, the wildflowers were a brilliant orange, the stream of water was ice blue, and the fish in the stream were literally rainbow trout, with all seven colors of a rainbow running down either side of their bodies.

As he kept walking he noticed a bright light off in the distance. It was so bright that he fancied for a moment he had found the sun's hiding place. But when he looked up above he could see through the branches that the sun was still floating in the sky and concluded that it couldn't be. Intrigued by the shining light he began to make his way toward it. As he got closer and closer it looked like it was a fire! It appeared as though flames of orange and yellow were swirling through the air, and so he began to run toward it to see if it was so. He was now about fifteen feet from the bright light and he was astonished, for, there was no smoke, nothing was burning. He could have sworn it was a fire, and yet no visible damage had been done to any of the surrounding trees or bushes. The yellow-orange light, however, was still shining splendidly. Intrigued, Asher crept closer and closer, and then he heard a voice ask, "Who's there?" The young man, startled, drew a deep breath. You would have thought that after the strange occurrences he had had earlier he wouldn't be so surprised. And yet so he was.

"Asher Svenson," he answered in a trembling tone.

"Hello, Asher," said the voice, "would you care to join me for some tea? I just gathered the leaves this morning." He was a bit shocked by such a gesture but warmly accepted the invitation.

"Why sure," he said, "that sounds lovely." He breathed a sigh of relief. He felt now that he wasn't in any danger. "Where are you, sir?" he asked, for he still couldn't see who was speaking.

"Over here!" said the voice. Asher was puzzled for a second. He looked around and around but did not see anyone.

"I don't see anyone," he finally replied.

"Come closer to the light," said the voice. Asher got as close as he could, and "hullo!" he shouted. It was a firefly!

"Greetings, Asher" the Firefly said. "I am so glad you decided to join me for tea. Here, let me dim my light a bit so you can see more clearly."

Asher started laughing out loud. "I beg your pardon, but I must tell you I feel rather embarrassed right now," he said while chuckling. "I saw your bright light from far off and I thought a fire was burning in the wood!" The Firefly was delighted to hear such a compliment.

"Well thank you," he said, "that is very kind of you to say."

"Come. I want to show you something," said Fai the Firefly. He flew in front of the young lad, his fiery light leading the way. He led him on a narrow dirt path. The density of the wood got thicker and thicker the further along the path they went. No longer were the trees spread out; they were packed tightly together, side by side, like stalks of corn in a cornfield. The path weaved around the trees such that it seemed like a maze. Then the ground started to gradually rise and Asher could tell they were ascending a hill. Fai was flying at a much quicker pace now and soon enough Asher lost sight of him. But he decided to press on and keep walking until he got to the top of the hill. As he was approaching the top of the hill the trees opened up and there was a small circular opening. All of a sudden a strange sensation overcame him. He felt like he had seen this place before but he couldn't recall where or when. He paused and looked around. Asher had forgotten that he was looking for the Firefly. Then all of a sudden right in front of him a bright light emerged. Fai had undimmed his light. And it was glowing so radiantly that Asher could no longer see him. He squinted his eyes and could only make out a glowing whiteness in front of him. Slowly it grew dimmer and he could start to make out a figure. The figure appeared to look like that of a man. But as the brightness from the light continued to decrease, he could more clearly see that it must be something other than a man. And to Asher's amazement, he realized it was an elf. The pointed ears are what gave it away. The elf looked like a king, as if he were the leader of a village of elves. He had chocolate brown skin and his hair was smooth and black, crowned with a wreath of golden leaves. He was dressed in dark blue attire with a brown leather strip coming diagonally across his jacket that was the strap of a bow, and on his left hip was a quiver of arrows. On his feet were light brown, paper-thin coverings that Asher figured must be some type of elfish sock or shoe which elves use to scale trees and mountains. There was a faint gleam of light still surrounding the elf's body.

With the twinkling of an eye the young man saw before him Fai turn from being a firefly into an elf. He could not believe it. Feelings of both fear and joy ran through him. Fai knew what he was thinking and said, "You are correct. I am both a firefly and an elf."

"Why didn't you tell me this earlier?" asked the young man.

"You would not have believed me even if I told you," said the Elf.

"But how is this even possible?" asked Asher. It was really a silly question, for he ought to have realized by now that such strange occurrences were normal in this wood.

But Fai was a very gracious elf, and so he answered, "Think of it like light. As quantum theory suggests, light can be both a wave and a particle. Its duality is mysterious and yet it is so."

Asher was delightfully surprised. "Ah! Quantum theory! I must admit that the interaction of subatomic particles is a most mysterious thing. It really is quite magical. Oh the wonders of science!"

Fai couldn't help but smile as the young man spoke with such glee. The two of them stood there in the opening of the wood and then Fai said, "I must get going soon, Asher."

"So soon?" asked the young man.

"It is my turn to keep watch over the wood," the Elf replied. Asher now realized why he had a bow and a quiver of arrows. "I must protect the wood and all who are in it."

Asher was sad to see Fai leave so soon, but he wished him well. "I bid you farewell, Noble Elf. I do hope I see you again."

"You will see me again," replied the Elf.

Asher moved on and set out to find a place to rest. He was exhausted. It was such a strange day that all he wanted to do was find a place to sit and stare up at the sky and look at the clouds as they moved along. He found a quiet spot and lay down with his hands behind his head, eyes closed, relaxing in the shaded area. He looked up at the large cumulonimbus clouds as they passed by and pondered the day's events, the conversations he had had with Mrs. Feathergloss, the Tree, and Fai. As troubled as he was by the day's occurrences, he felt unusually well. He realized that in the midst of all of these events there was inside of him much joy. It was an odd feeling. At the same time he felt like he was somewhere very far from home, and at other times it was like his adventure was more of a returning to a place he had visited long ago as a child. He was unsure of what it all meant. And so he continued to lie there in the shade, exhausted from the day's journey, and soon closed his eyes. A peace came over him that he had not felt in a long time. Then he fell asleep.

TALES OF COURAGE AND HOPE: BLACK PANTHER IN MIDDLE EARTH AND NARNIA

Seth Myers on the Connections from Oxford to Hollywood

How do we become good or evil?. . . All these philosophers are wrong, probably because most of them do not have children. Parents and children know the answer: by example. By having moral heroes.[1]

~ Peter Kreeft

---

[1] Peter Kreeft in Louis Markos, *On the Shoulders of Hobbits: the Road to Virtue with Tolkien and Lewis* (Grand Rapids, MI: Eerdmans, 2012), 8.

Recent blockbusters such as Broadway's 2015 musical *Hamilton* and Hollywood's 2018 film *Black Panther* offer us moral heroes and in particular, heroes from marginalized and minority communities. *Hamilton* relives the tale of the founding father, Alexander Hamilton, who was an orphaned immigrant to New York from the Caribbean island of Nevis and became the first US Secretary of the Treasury. In the hands of director Lin Manuel-Miranda, himself of Puerto Rican ancestry, Hamilton's story becomes the story of immigrants as much as of founding fathers. Blacks, Hispanics, and Asians are cast in nearly every role - except that of Britain's callous King George. We will look more closely at *Hamilton* in the companion article.

Black Panther is the Marvel Comic tale of an African superhero who must contend with militant countrymen over how to best share the resources and technology of the mythical African nation of Wakanda in order to alleviate the suffering and plight of one billion African brothers and sisters abroad. In the *Black Panther* galaxy, long, long ago the continent of Africa was the beneficiary of a meteor strike, which endowed it with a mountain of vibranium, the most advanced metal in the world. Five African tribes went to war over this metallic godsend, with four of the tribes uniting under a warrior who took on superhero powers when he learned to ingest it from a heart-shaped herb. Vibranium allowing them to develop technology and a society beyond the imagination of the rest of the world. Fearful of the powers granted them, these tribes decided to hide their discovery under the cover of a primitive African nation called Wakanda.

But *Black Panther* is more than simply a tale of technology and power politics; it is a story of choices. The choices are found in the contrast between two characters: the young king T'Challa and his cousin, who has his own lineal claim to the Wakandan throne. T'Challa follows the Wakandan party and wants to keep their resources secret, fearing how the outside world may handle such advances, while Stevens, who has spent his lifetime among the less advanced and oppressed diaspora Africans, seeks to empower them with vibranium so they might conquer their oppressors. The choice over whether to engage this fight, and the level of militancy with which to do so, is part of a more fundamental choice facing these Africans. They must also decide their identity - whether victim of the past or free moral agent - as well as grapple with the roles of the fathers in their lives.

Film, Story, and Myth – Some Philosophical and Theological Guides

The meaning we get from myth, and the significance we attribute to it, is a tale as old as humanity itself. The ancient stories and modern film are not so different. Philosophers have even been story-tellers. Even Plato's philosophizing against epic poetry could not stem this myth-making tide, for he has been described as one of the greatest practitioners of metaphorical myth-making. In the recent past, Umberto Eco and Ayn Rand have been known for their works in both philosophy and story-telling. Among Christian thinkers, the British are well known for their literary endeavors in explaining the Christian faith. We will include in our discussion perspectives from two Oxford Professors of Literature, C.S. Lewis (1898 - 1963) and his close friend, J.R.R. Tolkien (1892-1973). Lewis wrote extensively on literature of all ages, his Christian faith, and a number of fictional works, both fantasy and sci-fi; Tolkien is the author of *The Hobbit* and *The Lord of the Rings*, as well as several other works, and is considered to have revived the fantasy genre, in addition to his career as a world class philologist. In the companion *Black Panther* and *Hamilton* articles, we will compare the stories of *Black Panther* and *Hamilton* to each other as well as to insights from Lewis and Tolkien.[2]

Film is perhaps a more modern form of storytelling, and considering it as such has been a popular topic in recent years, particularly among Christian thinkers. In *Shows About Nothing*, Thomas Hibbs cites Nietzsche and DeTocqueville's concern that the freedom of a democratic society levels the field of truth claims to such an extent that nihilism results. Hibbs suggests that solutions to such nihilism can be found in works like Christopher Nolan's *Batman* where a hero battles chaotic evil or in the friendship and community of *Harry Potter*. Jeffrey Overstreet's *Through a Screen Darkly* shows how reflections of the goodness of God, as well as real evil, can be glimpsed at the movie theater. Similarly, in *Catching Light: Looking for God in the Movies*, Roy M. Anker helps us search for the Divine light that may seep through any good film. As Overstreet quotes Frederick Buechner, "The world

---

[2] Robert K. Johnston, "Evolution of Theology's Engagement with Film from Ethical Critique to Aesthetic Appropriation," *Reel Spirituality* (Grand Rapids, Michigan: Baker Academic, 2006), 56.

speaks of the holy in the only language it knows, which is a worldly language."[3] Finally, Robert K. Johnston looks at how theology and film inform each other in *Reel Spirituality: Theology and Film in Dialogue* (2006) and *Reel Spirituality* follows Johnston's 2004 *Useless Beauty: Ecclesiastes through the Lens of Contemporary Film.* In *Reel Spirituality*, Johnston shows how theology has historically tended to approach film from an ethical perspective but is increasingly partnering with films in appropriating and even finding divine encounters from an aesthetic perspective. It is by focusing on both ethics and aesthetics that we can view *Hamilton* and *Black Panther* through the lenses of Oxford dons like Lewis and Tolkien.

Fathers and Sons

The problem of fathers uninvolved in their children's lives is well understood in our modern culture of easy divorce, but in African American communities it is particularly acute. Ill-conceived if not racist societal and governmental factors also figure into the dissolution of the African-American family, as Ava DuVernay's critically acclaimed

---

[3] Frederick Buechner, *A Room to Remember* (1984) quoted in Jeffrey Overstreet, *Through a Screen Darkly* (Ventura, California: Regal Books, 2007), 5.

documentary film *13ᵗʰ* has recently argued. DuVernay exposes how the late-twentieth century "war on crime" has disproportionately targeted African-Americans and bloated the US prison system. In the documentary, figures such as Newt Gingrich, Bill Clinton, and Charlie Rangel agree that the manner of crime enforcement had devastating, if not at times intentional, consequences for African-American communities and families. DuVernay and others claim the consequences of "mass incarceration" resulted from what was initially a "war on drugs."

In *Black Panther*, T'Challa's and Killmonger's stories are largely shaped by those of their fathers. T'Challa's father, King T'Chaka, was the brother of Stevens' father, N'Jobu, who lived abroad as part of the Wakandan intelligence network. Early in the film, T'Chaka visits N'Jobu and confirms his suspicions that N'Jobu is pirating vibranium, even though N'Jobu appears to want to use it to empower oppressed Africans abroad. T'Chakah ends up killing N'Jobu while defending N'Jobu's assistant Zuri (who confesses their activities) from N'Jobu's attack. As a coverup, T'Chaka subsequently reports that N'Jobu has simply disappeared and leaves the young Stevens abroad to fend for himself. Stevens later attends MIT and the Naval Academy, becoming a special ops soldier who earns the title "Killmonger" and spends his life plotting his revenge and the capture of the Wakandan throne. As T'Challa states when later confronting his father over the matter, "(KIllmonger) is a monster of our own making . . . I must right these wrongs."

The fundamental difference between T'Challa's and Stevens' relationships with their fathers is made apparent by contrasting the trips each takes to "the ancestral zone" to converse with their late fathers. T'Chaka recounts to T'Challa how he had trained him side by side through his youth, hoping to fulfil the adage that "a man who has not prepared his children for his own death has failed as a father." T'Chaka offers the advice that even though T'Challa is "a good man with a good heart," he will need to surround himself with trustworthy companions. By contrast, Stevens' father N'Jobu regrets that he sacrificed young Erik's youth while on assignment rather than returning him to his native Wakanda.

The deeper challenges of the father-son relationships become evident as the sons decide how to handle their fathers' shortcomings. T'Challa decides he must right the wrongs of his father who helped to create the monster Killmonger, as well as reverse T'Chaka's failure to aid the globe's two billion struggling Africans. But the call to duty which beckons T'Challa is drowned out for Stevens who struggles to deal with his own identity. When questioned by N'Jobu about his lack of grief for his father, young Erik shows his growing cynicism by responding, "Everybody dies, that's just life around here." When N'Jobu expresses regrets that both father and son are abandoned, Killmonger points instead to the greater lostness of Wakanda.

Courage to Make the Right Choices

The crux of the question is how to move forward beyond their unjust past, and the answer is offered by the warrior and regiment leader Okoye, when she states, "you can't let your father's mistakes decide who you are. You get to decide what kind of king you are going to be."

Being responsible for your own choices is just one of the many virtues *Black Panther* offers as an alternative to Killmonger's vengeful ways. Just as the orcs state in Tolkien's *Lord of the Rings*, "Fear, the air is thick with it," the Wakandan air is thick with the scent of duty: from Okoye and Nakia's service to their country, to Okoye's prodding T'Challa to engage the challenge of offering their technology to the world, to T'Challa's sense of justice. In particular, T'Challa's courage stems from his deep sense of right and wrong, which contrasts with Killmonger's simple desire for vengeance and victory by providing their oppressed countrymen the opportunity to conquer their conquerors. This sense of justice and right and wrong, as well as the courage to follow it, also contrasts with some choices made by T'Chaka: "We let our fear of our discovery stop us from doing what was right," he admits, further adding that his sin to the young Stevens was a matter of regarding Erik as "the truth I chose to omit."

This courage to right injustices is an essential part of any solution. Courage seems to often be listed last when giving the four classical virtues: prudence (practical wisdom), moderation, justice, and fortitude (courage). But courage plays an essential role in all the preceding virtues. As Lewis observed in *Mere Christianity*, "you will notice, of course, that you cannot practice any of the other virtues very long without bringing this one (courage) into play."[4] But courage is not merely a Braveheart-styled "battle against unimaginable odds." As Lewis prefaced in the previous

---

[4] C.S. Lewis, *Mere Christianity* (New York: HarperOne, 2000), Book III Ch.2 "The Cardinal Virtues" p. 79.

observation, "fortitude includes both kinds of courage – the kind that faces as well as the kind that 'sticks it' under pain."[5] Thus, the courage of a Frodo and Samwise persevering on their lonely journey is on par with that of an Aragorn facing impossible odds in his battles against the orcs. Similarly, T'Challa's courage in battle is more than complemented by his courage in carrying out the long term program of compassionate sharing and education.[6]

The classical virtues that came from Plato's *Republic* were adopted by various writers of antiquity while Christian writers such as Augustine and Thomas Aquinas supplemented them with three cardinal virtues of faith, hope, and love. The term *cardinal* comes from the Latin *cardo* or hinge; thus, the virtuous life hinges on these three. A key distinction between classical and Christian virtues, however, is handily illustrated by Killmonger. It has been noted that the classical virtues, being on a par with Aristotle's notion of a "golden mean,"

---

[5] Ibid.

[6] Louis Markos, *On the Shoulders of Hobbits: the Road to Virtue with Tolkien and Lewis* (Chicago: Moody Publishers, 2012) further illustrates how courage and all the classical virtues can be seen in Tolkien's epic series, *The Lord of the Rings,* as well as in Lewis's own *Chronicles of Narnia.*

moderate between extremes of excess and deficiency. Thus, courage in its deficiency becomes cowardice and in its excess recklessness. Similarly, justice in its deficit can become injustice or cronyism, while in its excess vengeance. Theological virtues cannot be distorted in this way; while a lack of faith, hope or love may degenerate, there is no way to exhibit too much of these virtues. Too much love, or faith, or hope is never the problem; certainly, one cannot love too much. When Erik Stevens is moved by the injustices he sees outside of Wakanda (injustices T'Chaka and his generation were happy to ignore), he exercises his courage in order to do something about the situation. But at some point, he sought not simply to achieve something for the peoples who had been wronged, but to give them the technology to become conquerors themselves; it became a case of vengeance, an excess of the sense of justice.

Not only is courage necessary for the exercise of the other virtues, it often serves as the siren call to any virtue at all. In the *Screwtape Letters*, Lewis's demon schemer contends that "cowardice, alone of all the vices, is purely painful – horrible to anticipate, horrible to feel, horrible to remember . . . to make a wound deep in his charity, you should therefore first defeat his courage."[7] Opportunities for courage are in fact a divine godsend. Lewis continues, in the voice of Satan's apprentice, Screwtape:

> We have made men proud of most vices, but not of cowardice. Whenever we have almost succeeded in doing so, the Enemy permits a war or an earthquake or some other calamity and at once courage becomes so obviously lovely and important even in human eyes that all our work is undone . . . the undisguisable issue of cowardice or courage awakes thousands of men from moral stupor . . . in the last war, thousands of human, by discovering their own cowardice, discovered the whole moral world for the first time . . . This, indeed, is probably one of the Enemy's [God's] motives for creating a dangerous world – a world in which moral issues really come to the point. He sees as well as you do that ***courage is not simply one of the virtues, but the form of every virtue at the testing point, which means, at the point of highest reality. A chastity or honesty, or mercy, which yields to danger will be chaste or***

---

[7] C.S. Lewis, *Screwtape Letters* (New York: Harper Collins, 2000), Ch. 29, 160.

honest or merciful only on conditions. Pilate was merciful till it became risky."[8]

Wakanda and Women

The mythology of Wakanda does just that: the ever-present struggles of the wandering, displaced, and sinned-against races come back more savory to the viewer for having been dipped in the story of *Black Panther*. But it is not just the races and nations that are upheld in their struggles in *Black Panther*. There is a persistent theme of empowerment to the women of Wakanda. Not only is T'Challa's sister Shuri the chief technologist of Wakanda, but regiment leader Okoye (who seems destined to become Queen, though she has other ambitions) and Nakia offer strong, duty-driven, compassionate, and courageous role models. When T'Challa delivers his speech to the UN and is asked "with all due respect, what could a nation of farmers possibly have to offer the world", his confident grin of a response is shown only after Okoye and Nakia are seen similarly smiling about the unsuspecting contributions they may have to offer such a world.

---

[8] Ibid., 161.

Hope & Community: What's all the Courage for?

The Wakandan's sense of justice, compassion, and the courage to face their challenges ultimately culminates in hope. It is the look you see on the faces of both T'Challa and the young boy on the playground who asks T'Challa "who are you?" and on T'Challa, Okoye, and Nakia when asked what they might have to offer; it is a hope birthed with a sense of community and brotherhood. T'Challa states in his speech to the UN delegates (in a scene appearing halfway through the credits) that Wakanda intends to "work to be an example of how we as brothers and sisters on this earth should treat each other" and that "more connects us than separates us . . . we must find a way to look after one another as if we were one single tribe." This is offered in the midst of barely veiled references to the current climate: "in times of crisis, the wise build bridges while the foolish build barriers" and "now more than ever, the illusions of division threaten our very existence."

Tolkien considered the role of community, a village, so important that he placed the term "Fellowship" front and center in the title of the opening book of the *Lord of the Rings* saga, *The*

Fellowship of the Ring. The literary modernism of Tolkien's time, in many ways, was a reaction to the collapsed optimism of the 19th century as brought about by the Great War and was characterized by such lonely, introspective works as TS Eliot's poem *The Wasteland*, James Joyce's *Ulysses*, and Samuel Beckett's play "Waiting for Godot." Tolkien's rollicking, melancholic romance "is like lightning from a clear sky" according to Lewis, and "to say that in it heroic romance, gorgeous, eloquent, and unashamed, has suddenly returned at a period almost pathological in its anti-romanticism, is inadequate."[9] There is an innocence to Tolkien's Shire and race of Hobbits, a simple but happy folk for whom "growing food and eating it occupied most of their time" and who "in other matters they were, as a rule, generous and not greedy, but contented and moderate."[10] Even the warring Race of Men found a resource in such fellowship. As Aragorn observes of an attacking Orc, it is "in dark and loneliness they are strongest; they will not

---

[9] C.S. Lewis, "The Gods Return to Earth" in *Time and Tide* magazine, August 14, 1954, 1082. Online https://www.goodreads.com/quotes/504539-the-fellowship-of-the-ring-is-like-lightning-from-a accessed August 30, 2018.

[10] J.R.R. Tolkien, *The Fellowship of the Ring* (New York: Ballantine Books, 1980), 30.

openly attack a house where there are lights and many people."[11]

But this sense of fellowship draws on a much more ancient sense of community. The Christian doctrine of the Trinity, however mysterious and befuddling, offers the original paradigm of community. In speaking of the Trinity, St. Anselm of Canterbury in the 11th century noted how "the supreme spirit loves itself," how "each loves himself, and the other, with equal intensity" and how "one and the same love proceeds equally from Father and Son."[12] The Holy Spirit thus becomes, in this sense, the overflow of the love between God the Father and God the Son, sent to earth. Community and love are thus built into the DNA of the Triune Christian God. Not only does Jesus declare, "I no longer call you servants, but friends,"[13] but as Romans 8:17 reminds us, "Now if we are children, then we are heirs, heirs of God and co-heirs with Christ, if indeed we share in his sufferings in order that we may also share in his glory." It is this communion with God that the Christian faith

---

[11] Ibid., 236. Chapter I.10 "Strider."

[12] Anselm, *Monologion 49-51*, in *Anselm of Canterbury: The Major Works* (Oxford: Oxford University Press, 2008), 60-61.

[13] John 15:15

offers uniquely. Simpler monotheist deities simply demand worship rather than offer such inherent relationship. It is because we were made for this relationship with our Maker that we seek out relationships so intensely. As Augustine declared, "You have made us for yourself, and our hearts are restless until they find their rest in You."[14] Augustine thus hearkens to Scripture passages such as "God is love,"[15] reminding us that love requires someone doing the loving, someone being loved, as well as the love itself.

But what does community have to do with courage? T'CHalla, Okoye, Nakia, et. al. certainly draw on each other for strength and inspiration. But it is also a strong hope for a future community that inspires them. Tolkien made the case poetically, and one almost finds oneself in Middle Earth when reading the lines from his poem composed for Lewis, *Mythopoeia*:

Blessed are the timid hearts that evil hate,

that quail in its shadow, and yet shut the gate;

that seek no parley, and in guarded room,

through small and bare, upon a clumsy loom

weave issues gilded by the far-off day

---

[14] Augustine, *Confessions* I.1.

[15] 1 John 4:8, 16

hoped and believed in under Shadow's sway.

Blessed are the men of Noah's race that build
their little arks, though frail and poorly filled,
and steer through winds contrary towards a
wraith,
a rumour of a harbour guessed by faith.
 Blessed are the legend-makers with their
rhyme
of things nor found within record time.
It is not they that have forgot the Night . . .

Such isles they saw afar, and ones more fair,
and those that hear them yet may yet beware.
They have seen Death and ultimate defeat,
and yet they would not in despair retreat,
but oft to victory have turned the lyre
and kindled hearts with legendary fire,
illuminating Now and dark Hath-been
with light of suns as yet by no man seen.[16]

---

[16] J.R.R. Tolkien, *Mythpoeia*, 1931. A poem composed by Tolkien,
for Lewis, in which he tires to convince Lewis of the power of the
Christian story.
http://home.agh.edu.pl/~evermind/jrrtolkien/mythopoeia.htm.

Courage's Finale: A Song for History

Complementing the virtues of love and community, however, is that of courage and the hope it offers. T'Challa, Okoye, Nakia, and others embody courage, not just in summoning their strength in the face of fear to engage in dramatic battles, but in spending their strength over the long haul to aid their sisters and brothers. As a King, T'Challa embodies both the sudden burst of bravery as well as the temper to carry out his vision over the long haul. And he does it with a smile, as we see at the end. Such confident but joyful optimism is characteristic of a King. Lewis is helpful yet again, as he has been shown to employ the imagery of Jupiter, the King of the Planets, to describe the reign of Aslan in his Narnia series.

> We may say [Jupiter] is Kingly, but we must think of a King at peace, enthroned, taking his leisure, serene. The Jovial character is cheerful, festive, yet temperate, tranquil, magnanimous. When this planet dominates we may expect halcyon days and prosperity.[17]

---

[17] C.S. Lewis, *The Discarded Image* (Cambridge: Cambridge University Press, 1995), 106. The passage is quoted in Michael Ward, Planet Narnia: The Seven Heavens in the Imagination of C.S. Lewis (New York: Oxford University Press, 2008), 43. The 10th anniversary

Lewis' Aslan character in the *Chronicles of Narnia* leads both in warfare and celebration; and even the palace of the Kings and Queens of Narnia, Cair Paravel, is said to look like "a great star resting on the seashore."[18]

Tolkien strikes similar kingly postures. Aragorn from Tolkien's *Lord of the Rings* embodies just such Kingship:

> Thus he became at last the most hardy of living Men, skilled in their crafts and lore, and was yet more than they; for he was elven wise, and there was a light in his eyes that when they were kindled few could endure. His face was sad and stern because of the doom that was laid on him, and yet hope dwelt ever in the

of Ward's book, identifying a particular planet's imagery with each of the seven books of The Chronicles of Narnia (with interactions in his sci-fi Space Trilogy as well) is the theme of the December, 2018 *Unexpected Journal*. Ward first made the planetary connection when reading Lewis' poem The Planets in which themes of various Chronicles of Narnia books aligned with the poem's planetary. Lewis' The Planets may be found in C.S. Lewis, Poems (New York: Harcourt, 1992), and at http://www.pacificaoc.org/wp-content/uploads/Planets.pdf; Ward's site is www.planetnarnia.com.

[18] C.S. Lewis, *The Lion, the Witch and the Wardrobe* (New York: Harper Collins, 1994), 142. Ch.12. Ward mentions this in the condensed, more popular level reading version of his *Planet Narnia* (which was his dissertation): *The Narnia Code* (Carol Stream, Ill.: Tyndale House, 2010), 56.

depths of his heart, from which mirth would arise at times like a spring from the rock.[19]

But the sense of kingship found in Lewis and Tolkien have a common, ancient, and yet contemporary, root: it is based in Christ. While Lewis was content to place the enduring kingship of Narnia in the lion Aslan (son of the Emperor over the sea), a Christ figure, Tolkien scattered his Christological symbols throughout his story. The above passage on Aragorn, heir to the throne of Gondor, hearkens not just to a king, but a savior, a King like Jesus, fully man, yet fully God, who is "more than" the race of living Men, a King like Jesus with "a light in his eyes that few could endure" which reminds us of the description of Jesus in the Book of Revelation with "eyes blazing like fire,"[20] a King like Jesus who knew sorrow mixed with mirth. This is the model for Kingship to which T'Challa ultimately kneels though he follows in his own humble but confident way there.

---

[19] J.R.R. Tolkien, *Return of the King* (New York: Ballantine Books, 1994), 374. Appendix A.5.

[20] Revelation 19:12-13. The verse continues, affirming the identity of this rider on the white horse as Christ the King.

T'Challa's counterpart, Killmonger, shows a lack of such courage, especially in his final scene. His voice reflects the anguish of not just his own generation but that of his ancestors as well. He rejects the offer of restoration from his wounds, fearing it will simply lead to a life of imprisonment. Killmonger then proceeds to powerfully connect his plight with that of his ancestors in his final words: "Bury me at sea, like my ancestors who jumped from slave ships because they knew death is better than a life of bondage."

But it may not be entirely fair to criticize Killmonger for a lack of heart and a failure of courage. By definition, courage is summoned in battling the unfavorable odds, and sometimes the house wins. Stevens has perhaps, finally and mortally, wearied of the battle. Continued rejection, rejection held against the memories of what family, tribe and nation had hoped for you, takes its toll. At such times, the dream stays alive by taking it to heart, and telling the story to the next generation. That is what Stevens does. It is nearly the entire theme of Hamilton as we will see: the story of forgotten founding father Alexander Hamilton repeats the refrain "Who lives? Who dies? Who tells your story?" For Black Panther, the story reaches into the past, but looks expectantly and courageously into the future.

Hope, Life, and the Fountain of Trevi

Carla Alvarez on the Power of Water

Visitors from all over the world are drawn to the city of Rome and among all of the city's historical and artistic sites, one of the biggest draws is the Fountain of Trevi. A visit to the city is simply not complete if one has not visited and tossed their coins into the fountain.

The site is familiar to those who have never visited Rome. It has been filmed in several movies such as *La Dolce Vita* (The Sweet Life)[1] and *Three Coins in a Fountain*. In the latter, the fountain is a focal point of the plot line and includes the legend that claims if one tosses three coins over the left shoulder into the fountain, the person will return

---

[1] *La Dolce Vita*, directed by Federico Fellini (Cineriz, 1960), accessed September 17, 2015,
http://www.imdb.com/title/tt0053779/.

to Rome and find their true love.[2] It is a place where hopes are fulfilled.

There is a sense of peace and a desire to linger when walking near the fountain. People can be found sitting around the fountain at any hour of the day. It is a meeting place; a place where if a wish is made, that wish will come true.

Where does this sense of hope come from? Looking at the images in the sculpture, at first glance one would think it was created in the pre-Christian era of the Roman Empire. It was not. It was actually created by Nicola Salvi through a commission of Pope Clement XII in 1730 AD. Neither Clement nor Salvi lived to see the full design of the project to completion. All of the elements of the design were finally finished and the fountain inaugurated on May 22, 1762 AD.[3]

While the current fountain was designed in the 18th century, various fountains have been at the site since shortly before the time of Christ. The earliest legend of the site tells us that in 19 BC a virgin led weary Roman soldiers to the spot where

---

[2] *Three Coins in the Fountain*, Directed by Jean Negulesco (20th Century Fox, 1954), accessed September 17, 2015, http://www.imdb.com/title/tt0047580/.

[3] "History," *The Trevi Fountain*, accessed September 17, 2015, http://www.trevifountain.net/trevifountainhistory3.htm.

they found fresh water. An aqueduct was built from this spot to bring water to the city. Later, the Church of St. Ignatius was built at this location.[4]

Plain prophecies were given to the Jewish people to watch for the Redeemer of Yahweh, who chose them as his own people. However, embedded in the myths of every culture are hints and promises of God. Some were more explicit like the sayings of the Greek Sibylline Oracles. Others, like the legend were a hint and a foreshadowing. As the virgin Mary brought forth the Savior of the world, a virgin leads the weary to the source of fresh and ever flowing water.[5][6]

Salvi designed Ocean to be the focal point of the scene who is "the personification of an immense river that flows around the earth and from which all streams of water derive."[7] Water represents life and the Holy Spirit in the Bible. One of the most dramatic visions in the Bible was written by John in his Revelation; John describes a river of the water of life flowing from the throne of God.[8] This fountain

---

[4] Ibid.

[5] Matthew 11:28-29.

[6] John 4:14.

[7] "Iconography," *The Trevi Fountain,* accessed September 17, 2015, http://www.trevifountain.net/iconography.htm.

[8] Revelation 22:1.

could be a depiction of that vision with Ocean triumphing over all who oppose him and his never ending flood of justice going before him.[9]

On either side of Ocean stand Abundance and Health; they follow behind in his victory. As Jesus, the giver of living water said, "I come that you might have life, and have it more abundantly."[10] He suffered a tortuous whipping to pay the price for our healing.[11] The redemption of Christ is not just of spirit in the distant future, but a reclaiming and restoration in the here and now.

The scene is a visual depiction of the power won at the cross and brought onto earth at the resurrection. We read the verses, but do we understand the shaking that went on when the sun went dark and the curtain was rent? The warring horses led by tritons over the tumult of the water echo the sense of that power.

In the middle of the depths of depression, David wrote in Psalm 42 "Deep calls to deep in the roar of your waterfalls."[12] Water speaks to us. Even if we are not looking for God, He speaks to us by water. It

---

[9] Amos 5:24.

[10] John 10:10b.

[11] Isaiah 53:5.

[12] Psalm 42:7

brings forth a stillness, a wanting to connect. Before God breathed life into Adam, his spirit hovered over the surface of the water.[13]

Water is a symbol of life and of new beginnings. Jesus said that whoever believes in him "from his innermost being will flow rivers of living water." (John 7:38) It is a representation of that life eternal, a wellspring that will never run dry. This magnificent fountain is a physical depiction of the force of that desire. The Trevi Fountain brings a sense of homecoming and a looking forward to full and complete restoration - a day when war has ceased and strife and contention is no more.

---

[13] Genesis 1:2.

THE LORD OF THE RINGS AND CONSOLATION CONCERNING DEATH

Jason Monroe on the Central Theme of J. R. R. Tolkien's Masterpiece

Along with the fear of heights and of public speaking, *thanatophobia* — the fear of death — usually makes most Top Ten Fears lists. Given the grim statistic that one out of every one person dies, death is commonly either greatly feared or greatly ignored. Interestingly, according to some religions, a few men have not died. Others even claim that some have come back to life. The possibility of resurrection can inspire hope in the face of death, but still the customary cloud of dread does not always readily dissipate. Helpful knowledge may assuage worry, but no one can visit death experimentally to retrieve data for the living. So what can be done to bring consolation? Well, we can tell good stories. Stories (especially fairy tales) thematically featuring death are invaluable in positively processing it. Michael Miller notes, "Fairy tales and other good stories set out a moral universe, and they teach truth about reality."[1] According to J.R.R. Tolkien, they speak to "the oldest and deepest desire, the Great Escape: the Escape from Death."[2] *The Lord of the Rings*[3] is a fairy tale *par excellence* and "is about something much more permanent and difficult: Death and Immortality."[4] Given this helpful revelation by Tolkien and the book's status as a respected and loved fairy tale, *LOTR* can be extremely beneficial in finding consolation when confronting death.

Encountering death in fantasy or fairy stories can help one come to terms with his own mortality. In "On Fairy-stories," Tolkien notes, "it is one of the lessons of fairy-stories (if we can speak of the lessons of things that do not lecture) that on callow,

---

[1] Michael Miller, "C. S. Lewis, Scientism, and the Moral Imagination," in *The Magician's Twin*, ed. John G. West (Seattle: Discovery Institute Press, 2012), 327.

[2] J.R.R. Tolkien, *On Fairy-stories*, eds. Verlyn Flieger and Douglas A. Anderson (London: Harper Collins, 2008), 74.

[3] "*LOTR*" from here on.

[4] J.R.R. Tolkien, *The Letters of J.R.R. Tolkien*, ed. Humphrey Carpenter (New York: Houghton Mifflin, 2000), 246.

lumpish, and selfish youth peril, sorrow, and the shadow of death can bestow dignity, and even sometimes wisdom."[5] Tolkien did not by any means intend *LOTR* to be allegorical,[6] but in many ways, readers can be comforted in sympathizing with the characters' responses to death. Many people acknowledge that suffering and struggle can refine one's character and assist him in his journey toward maturation. This applies also to the imagination. Readers can relate to characters like Gandalf, Sam, and Pippin as they show resolve and courage when all hope seems lost.

In word and deed, the wizard Gandalf aptly responds to the common complaint, "Life's not fair!" He admonishes Frodo: "Many that live deserve death. And some that die deserve life."[7] He not only addresses this paradox, he lives it by dying for the Company of the Ring in his battle with the Balrog. He is a good character and did not by any means deserve death. However, his sacrifice provides clues to unravelling the injustice many ascribe to death. Can it ever be inherently redemptive? Gandalf's

---

[5] Tolkien, *On Fairy-stories*, 59.

[6] Tolkien, *The Letters of J.R.R. Tolkien*, 41.

[7] J.R.R. Tolkien, *The Fellowship of the Ring* (New York: Houghton Mifflin, 1994), 58.

sacrifice seems to imply "yes," given his resurrection as the more powerful Gandalf the White. Additionally, he helps the Company along toward destroying the Ring. His selflessness can be encouraging when wrestling with the idea that survival may not be Man's highest goal. Perhaps reality has something deeper and richer about it that calls for one to "lay down one's life for one's friends."[8]

In *LOTR*, the good characters recognize virtue in fighting against Sauron, who is threatening their beloved homeland. They realize the necessity of warring to save their way of life, given the alternative of either slavery or death (or both) at Sauron's hand. Servitude would not be much of a life: the oppression would be so bad as to remove any chance of a satisfactory day-to-day existence. Faced with the alternative of surrendering or fighting, the latter would be a for a higher cause. Elrond, speaking of Isildur, says that death may not be the worst-case scenario: "Yet death maybe was better than what else might have befallen him."[9] Even amid deathly fears, this realization gives courage and comfort to those fighting to destroy

---

[8] John 15:13 (NABRE).

[9] Tolkien, *The Fellowship of the Ring*, 237.

the Ring. As Pippin loses consciousness in battle, his thought reacts to what appears his passing from life: "'So it ends as I guessed it would,' his thought said, even as it fluttered away; and it laughed a little within him ere it fled, almost gay it seemed to be casting off at last all doubt and care and fear."[10] Something from deep within Pippin recognizes the good life; a life worth fighting and (possibly) dying for gives him a worthy aim. Becoming immersed in the magic of the story, a reader can relate to Pippin's position. Someone fighting to preserve the Good in our Primary World[11] can be encouraged by the positive shift in Pippin's perspective.

Elven wrestlings with immortality can, in a way, sympathize with human worries about death. "As for the Elves. . . . The Elves were sufficiently longeval to be called by Man 'immortal'. But they were not unageing or unwearying."[12] Usually, immortality means either the soul's capacity to survive the body's death or it indicates the body's power to live forever. Tolkien imagines the elves to be "confined to the limits of this world (in space

---

[10] J.R.R. Tolkien, *The Return of the King* (New York: Houghton Mifflin, 1994), 874.

[11] Tolkien uses this term to refer to our real world, in contrast to the Secondary World of the sub-creator.

[12] Tolkien, *The Letters of J.R.R. Tolkien*, 325.

and time), even if they died, and would continue in some form to exist in it until 'the end of the world'."[13] Normally, elves would live as long as the world lasted. If killed, they could be reincarnated: "After a certain period of time and rest, their spirits (*fear*) are incarnated in bodies (*hroar*) identical to their old ones."[14] Slain elves first go to the Halls of Mandos — the Halls of Waiting — before the Valar approve their reunion to the body. Thus elves are perpetually linked, in one way or another, to the world until its end. It is understandable if the repetition of worldly cycles causes grief or weariness in the elves. But those responding to their situations in positive ways (Galadriel resisting temptation to power or Legolas humbly befriending Gimli) can hugely encourage readers who may carry burdens of their own. By maintaining in their lives a robust sense of wonder and adventure, elves can bring hope to those who may have lost it.

The juxtaposition of the natural fates of elves and men can provide a fresh perspective on immortality and mortality. An indefinite life span

---

[13] Ibid., 325.

[14] "Elven Life Cycle," *Tolkien Gateway*, accessed October 20, 2016, http://tolkiengateway.net/wiki/Elven_Life_cycle.

must feel much different than a definite one. To the elves, the finitude of men's lives "meant 'liberation from the circles of the world', and is in that respect to them enviable."[15] Readers can place themselves in the elves' shoes, pondering the possibilities of living indefinitely: how would an endless experience of Earth's ages and epochs feel? Children and grandchildren are blessings, but to meet ten, twenty, or more generations of them? The experience could be strange, monotonous, and may evoke the question, "Where does lasting happiness originate? Is it only to be found on Earth?" These questions could magnify the futility of seeking fulfilment only in temporal things. The longing, therefore, for "something more" may grow more acute, and God would start to seem for the soul what food is for the body — a necessity.

Immortality can be imagined to be good and peaceful — not unbearable like a continuous carnival, conceivably causing suffering. Discontent of immortality manifests in how some atheists view heaven. Atheists tend to liken heaven to a "celestial theme park"[16] — a constant churning of

---

[15] Tolkien, *The Letters of J.R.R. Tolkien*, 325.

[16] Tim Claason, "There is No Benign Religion," *Tim Stepping Out*, May 22, 2015, accessed June 12, 2018,

mediocre complacence, soon becoming nothing short of Chinese Water Torture. Failing to imagine a qualitative improvement in heavenly consciousness, they imagine heaven as an eternal bore. It is true that no one can fully fathom the afterlife: the elves also did not know what "'the end of the world' portended."[17] But this did not make thoughts of the afterlife terrifying or insipid. At the close of *LOTR*, those sailing for Aman (the Undying Lands), "left the physical world,"[18] and the "sojourn was a 'purgatory', but one of peace and healing and they would eventually pass away (*die* at their own desire and of free will) to destinations of which the Elves know nothing."[19] Aman is not Middle Earth's equivalent of heaven (its mortal visitors do not become immortal). It can, nevertheless, help one imagine heaven because it is the home of the Valar — good, powerful angelic beings who make it the "Blessed Realm."[20] The purgatorial transformation of those in-transit can represent becoming holy to

---

https://timsteppingout.wordpress.com/2015/05/22/there-is-no-benign-religion/.

[17] Tolkien, *The Letters of J.R.R. Tolkien*, 325.

[18] Ibid., 411.

[19] Ibid., 411.

[20] Ibid., 205.

enter heaven. The believability — what Tolkien terms "the inner consistency of reality"[21] — of *LOTR* makes the characters' peace and acceptance seem realistic and coherent with the rest of the story. Therefore, their last journey can inspire faith in the goodness and peace of heaven.

Another principle of good stories is that ruin results for those who reject their natural fate and grasp for what they pridefully deem a better alternative. In Middle Earth's history, Sauron manipulates the mortal King Ar-pharazon to war against the "Blessed Realm [Aman] itself, and wrest it and its 'immortality' into his own hands."[22] But the king's improper groping for immortality is "wicked because 'unnatural', and silly because Death in that sense is the Gift of God (envied by the Elves), release from the weariness of Time."[23] In Tolkien's myth, "Death – the mere shortness of human life span – is not a punishment for the Fall, but a biologically (and therefore also spiritually, since body and spirit are integrated) inherent part of Man's nature."[24] Ar-pharazon's folly

---

[21] Tolkien, *On Fairy-stories*, 59.

[22] Tolkien, *The Letters of J.R.R. Tolkien*, 205.

[23] Ibid., 205.

[24] Ibid., 205.

consequently precipitates the destruction of the great land of Numenor. If he had viewed death as a gift from his creator this calamity could have been avoided. Instead, he attempted to overcome death in his own way, on his own terms. Once again, Tolkien's Secondary World urges acceptance and wise preparation for the unavoidable deadline of natural death.

Sam Gamgee's loyalty is a great example of keeping courage and hope when all seems lost. Overcome by fear and helplessness, Sam resolutely retains a sense of duty: "'So that was the job I felt I had to do when I started,' thought Sam: 'to help Mr. Frodo to the last step and then die with him? Well, if that is the job then I must do it."[25] Sam's firm determination stems from a commitment to his master, Frodo. Morality informs his mortality— duty unto death. Unlike Gollum, who waives good will in order to survive, Sam's good nature prompts him to keep his promises, even in extreme peril. A Primary World manifestation of Sam's resolve is a soldier fiercely fighting for freedom. He embraces possible death with steeled face and unwavering will. Pain and terror may assail him, but they need not dominate, drowning him in despair. Bombs or

---

[25] Tolkien, *The Return of the King*, 913.

bullets may be at any turn, but he can make ready his soul. In *LOTR*, many face death with courage and hope. Sam's staying true to duty is an example of how one can prepare for death.

Conversely, Saruman selfishly asserts himself and desires undue power and personal safety. Unlike those mentioned above who would rather die than serve Sauron, Saruman "wishes to be the Lord and God of his private creation. He will rebel against the laws of the Creator – especially against mortality. Both of these (alone or together) will lead to the desire for Power, for making the will more quickly effective, – and so to the Machine (or Magic)."[26] Because his will is bent enough, Saruman will employ whatever means necessary to save his own skin. This and the ulterior motive to gain the Ring drive him to align with Sauron. In the long run, these choices begin to warp his mind and motivations: "He has a mind of metal and wheels; and he does not care for growing things. . ."[27] Opting to be the artificer of a megalomaniacal orc-powered machine, he uses magic for malevolence. The elves use magic (their Art) for "product, and

---

[26] Tolkien, *The Letters of J.R.R. Tolkien*, 145.

[27] J.R.R. Tolkien, *The Two Towers* (New York: Houghton Mifflin, 1994), 616.

vision in unflawed correspondence;"[28] Saruman, wanting to conquer death and nature, uses it for "domination and tyrannous re-forming of Creation."[29]

Both elves and men can either accept their natural fates contentedly or try to circumvent them unreasonably. Inescapably, the latter leads to peril if pursued long enough. This parallels sin in the Primary World: to desire what someone thinks good for him, while rejecting the good things God has willed results in a distancing from God. In *LOTR*, submitting fully to the will of the Creator is pivotal to having a strong character. If one submits to God, he follows Tolkien's good characters, ultimately improving his life. By not grasping at unnaturally long life, he will feel more fulfilment. John Garth highlights this axiom of Faerie: "Enchantment, as we know from fairy-tale traditions, tends to slip away from envious eyes and possessive fingers . . ."[30] Stories can exemplify obedience to God which stabilizes stray strands in Man's fallenness. Sin will affect Man until the end

---

[28] Tolkien, *The Letters of J.R.R. Tolkien*, 146.

[29] Ibid., 146.

[30] John Garth, *Tolkien and the Great War: The Threshold of Middle-earth* (New York: Mariner, 2005), chap. 4, iBooks.

of time, but by living properly to his created nature, his soul will be renewed daily — not descending toward decay, like Saruman's.

Not all in Middle Earth are involuntarily fixed with mortality or immortality: the "half-elven" may choose. Arwen is given the chance "to divest herself of 'immortality' and become 'mortal.'"[31] Toward the end of *LOTR*, Arwen does not accompany those departing for the Undying Lands. She says, "For mine is the choice of Luthien, and as she so have I chosen, both the sweet and the bitter."[32] Her choice is bitter, separating her from Elrond: ("the grief at her parting from Elrond is specially poignant"[33]); simultaneously, it's sweet because she can be with Aragorn. As she promises, "I will cleave to you, Dunadan, and turn from the Twilight,"[34] she is realizing her own desire that is stronger than that for immortality. She mirrors the martyr or soldier who would die for a higher cause. Her love for Aragorn becomes a worthwhile reason to choose mortality. As the good characters in the story would rather die than live an imitation life

---

[31] Tolkien, *The Letters of J.R.R. Tolkien*, 193.

[32] Tolkien, *The Return of the King*, 952.

[33] Tolkien, *The Letters of J.R.R. Tolkien*, 193.

[34] Tolkien, *The Return of the King*, 1036.

under Sauron, so Arwen would rather live a mortal life with Aragorn than spend indefinite days alone. How packed is literature's past with stories of love that defy death? The impact of Romeo and Juliet would be much different if their love wasn't strong enough to die for. Good stories can bring this point home with passion and poetic beauty that other mediums lack.

The One Ring contributes to the theme under consideration by unnaturally increasing the wearer's life span and thereby providing its own (albeit counterfeit) consolation. "The chief power (of all the rings alike) was the prevention and slowing of *decay* (i.e. 'change' viewed as a regrettable thing), the preservation of what is desired or loved, or its semblance. . ."[35] To anyone desiring preservation of his life's goods, acquiring the Ring would seem serendipitous, "for it gave long life."[36] But there is more to the Ring than meets the eye. It inexorably consumes Gollum, as drink does an alcoholic; even Bilbo also has difficulty parting with it in Hobbiton. One cannot possess It without It eventually possessing him. The Ring, like some sin, does not seem so bad at

---

[35] Tolkien, *The Letters of J.R.R. Tolkien*, 152.

[36] Tolkien, *The Fellowship of the Ring*, 58.

first since it could be used to save one's life or the lives of his friends. Tolkien mentions that it is "more or less an Elvish motive"[37] to want to preserve desirables. But a difference exists between using corrupt, artificial means to preserve life and submitting to the natural Source of life. Many disregard the moral chasm yawning between the two. As Tolkien's story shows, despair awaits those devising to be gods of their destiny. Trusting in the Creator's design, however, brings peace and joy, regardless of length of life.

Good stories and fairy tales can sympathize with the not unreasonable fear of dying: they can help anyone find lasting peace about it. Tolkien reminds us that stories are extremely valuable, providing "consolation" and "the imaginative satisfaction of ancient desires."[38] Good stories foster joy of a particular quality most helpful in fulfilling primordial longings, such as that of transcending death. Without this joy, one is much more susceptible to life's pitfalls and temptations. Sauron, due to his bloated desire for power and immortality, was blind to the approach of Frodo and Sam. He would never have guessed it possible

---

[37] Tolkien, *The Letters of J.R.R. Tolkien*, 152.

[38] Tolkien, *On Fairy-stories*, 75.

that such meekness could be his undoing. Because his ambition blinded him from the deepest powers at work in his world, he was in due course defeated. This sudden, breathtaking triumph of good over evil is the "Consolation of the Happy Ending,"[39] which Tolkien considered essential to good stories. Those open to its heart-changing effects will glimpse the world's most profound power — that of selfless Love. Frodo and Sam set the example by embarking on a quest to save their beloved people and country, despite mortal danger. Eventually they tap into immortal truths which are as distant to Sauron as the East is from the West.

---

[39] Ibid., 75.

THE HEROISM OF THE ORDINARY IN THE LORD OF THE RINGS

Zak Schmoll on the character of Samwise Gamgee

G.K. Chesterton defended the value of fairy tales as he wrote *Orthodoxy*. Specifically, he wrote, "Fairyland is nothing but the sunny country of common sense. It is not earth that judges heaven, but heaven that judges earth; so for me at least it was not earth that criticized Elfland, but Elfland that criticized the earth."[1] Even though some may dismiss these fantasy stories as childish, fairyland can be used as an effective tool to illustrate truths about the world we inhabit. Those stories can illuminate our story. In *The Lord of the Rings*, J.R.R.

---

[1] G.K Chesterton, *Orthodoxy* (Chicago: Moody Press, 2009), 76, Kindle Edition.

Tolkien used his own personal fairyland to show the true heroism in the ordinary.

Samwise Gamgee, a gardener by trade, was thrust into an adventure he was not looking for. Interestingly, he was referred to by Tolkien in a letter to publisher Milton Waldman as, "the chief hero."[2] In a story of epic proportions full of good and evil, this may be a somewhat surprising admission from Tolkien. Gandalf, Aragorn, or Frodo might seem to be more reasonable choices for this most prominent position given their centrality to the narrative at large. In fact, these three characters have been highlighted by scholars such as Donald Williams who points out in his book *An Encouraging Thought*, that each one can be seen as symbolic of the different offices of Jesus Christ. Gandalf seems to represent the role of the priest, Aragorn points to the role of King, and Frodo qualifies as the suffering servant. "Gandalf; Frodo; Aragorn: None of these characters is exactly a Christ figure in the full sense of that phrase, though perhaps cumulatively they add up to one."[3]

---

[2] J.R.R. Tolkien, *The Letters of J.R.R. Tolkien*, ed. Humphrey Carpenter (New York: Houghton Mifflin Harcourt, 2013), Kindle Location 3391, Kindle Edition.

[3] Donald Williams, *An Encouraging Thought: The Christian Worldview in the Writings of J. R. R. Tolkien* (Cambridge, Ohio:

However, one of the most powerful, yet surprisingly hidden, themes in *The Lord of the Rings* emerges because of this authorial decision to make the humble the "chief hero" rather than any of these three. Tolkien is showing that it is indeed heroic to be an ordinary person in an ordinary town who does whatever he or she can to make a small corner of the world a better place. It is Tolkien's entrance into fairyland that invites us to follow and discover why the ordinary can be heroic in his world. In our world, that almost seems to be a contradiction in terms as we become numb to our typical environment. However, in this fantastical environment, we learn the truth, and we realize it makes sense not only in Middle Earth where we see it, but in our own world as well where we want to see it.

The destruction of the Ring might seem to be the most important event in this story, the ultimate heroic act. It is seemingly the entire purpose of the quest that caused Frodo and Sam to leave the Shire in the first place. The main problem with that hypothesis is that evil is not destroyed when the Ring fell into the fire with Gollum. The four hobbits

---

Christian Publishing House, 2018), Kindle Locations 415-416, Kindle Edition.

return with Gandalf to find their hometown in disrepair and under the thumb of the evil wizard Saruman.

Gandalf then provides a tantalizing hint towards the true purpose of *The Lord of the Rings* right before he leaves the hobbits at the entrance to this Shire that is no longer recognizable. Merry laments that Gandalf cannot join them and help them free their homeland, but Gandalf encourages them in their own ability. "I am not coming to the Shire. You must settle its affairs yourselves; that is what you have been trained for."[4]

This is a highly significant revelation because Gandalf is implying that the entire journey to destroy the Ring has only been preparation for this, the real mission facing the hobbits. The hobbits need to become the heroes that rescue their ordinary homeland. Stratford Caldecott hypothesizes that this training is vital for the hobbits to be able to handle what they now have to face in the reclamation of their homeland.

> The success of the hobbits in dealing with this final peril would not have been possible—would certainly not have been

---

[4] J.R.R. Tolkien, *The Lord of the Rings: One Volume* (New York: Houghton Mifflin Harcourt, 2002), 996, Kindle Edition.

believable—if they had not experienced the epic adventure as a whole, and if we had not seen them transformed into heroes of song and legend; so that when they are plunged back into the banality of the Shire they are able to defeat the evil that they find with the grace—the gifts— that they have received in their travels.[5]

We must always keep in mind who specifically the Shire was saved for because it certainly was not saved for all four hobbits. They do not all return to ordinary lives. Frodo, because of his injuries, realizes that Middle Earth is no longer his home. He tells Sam before his departure from Middle Earth, "I tried to save the Shire, and it has been saved, but not for me."[6] The Shire is similarly not saved for Merry and Pippin. With the former having pledged service to the kingdom of Rohan and the latter to the kingdom of Gondor, their destinies also stretch beyond the borders of their natural home. The only one to return to his hometown and remain was Sam who finishes the tale with the line, "Well, I'm

---

[5] Stratford Caldecott, *The Power of the Ring: The Spiritual Vision Behind the Lord of the Rings and The Hobbit* (New York: The Crossroad Publishing Company, 2012), Kindle Locations 907-911, Kindle Edition.

[6] Tolkien, *The Lord of the Rings,* 1029, Kindle Edition.

back."[7] The Shire was saved, and it was saved for Sam, the author's chief hero.

If that is true and the true purpose of the story was to save the Shire specifically for the hero, Sam, then the inevitable question is, "What makes Sam specifically heroic?" What about his character makes him worthy of such an extraordinary position as "chief hero" among a group of mighty warriors from around Middle Earth? Why is Sam the hero when there are heavy Christlike references made to multiple other characters as shown by Williams? Sam begins the story as ordinary, and he finishes the story as ordinary.

In the first dialogue of *The Fellowship of the Ring*, Sam's father Hamfast shares some advice with his friends that he claims to have told Sam. "Elves and Dragons! I says to him. Cabbages and potatoes are better for me and you. Don't go getting mixed up in the business of your betters, or you'll land in trouble too big for you, I says to him."[8] This attitude is somewhat apparent in Sam, but there is some other desire embedded as well. "He had a good deal to think about. For one thing, there was a lot to do up in the Bag End garden, and he would have a

---

[7] Ibid., 1032.

[8] Ibid., 24.

busy day tomorrow, if the weather cleared. The grass was growing fast. But Sam had more on his mind than gardening."[9] Immediately before this passage, Sam had been having a conversation with a fellow hobbit about dragons and elves. He is attentive to the mundane, just like his father advised he ought to be to avoid trouble, but he also has his mind set on things beyond the Shire. What other people write off as foolishness, he desires to encounter and experience.

Sam returns to his home alone at the end of the book to settle down with his family. In one of his final lines, Frodo says, "It must often be so, Sam, when things are in danger: someone has to give them up, lose them, so that others may keep them. But you are my heir: all that I had and might have had I leave to you."[10] Not only does this provide further support to the idea that this entire mission was really about saving the Shire for Sam, but it also provides a type of theodicy. All of the evil that Frodo had to go through contributed to this end. Frodo had to suffer in order for the Shire to be saved. All of the evil that Aragorn, Gandalf, Eowyn,

---

[9] Ibid., 45.

[10] Ibid., 1029.

and even Boromir went through contributed to the saving of the Shire for the hero, Sam.

Danger looms at the beginning of the journey, and if the mission had never taken place, the forces of evil would have eventually triumphed. Eventually the Ring would have been found, and evil would have claimed victory once and for all. It was mentioned many times that they could not simply hide the Ring and hope it was never found. It had to be destroyed. Therefore, the evil that each of these people had to face had meaning. Evil things were allowed to happen in the lives of these characters because they provided the training that brought the triumph of the hero. Evil brought Sam, the hero, to the place where he belonged, the ordinary. Being secure in that place indeed is what made him the hero.

This entrance into fairyland allows us to see an ordinary gardener become the hero after overcoming great evil. On earth, each one of us may be that simple person who wonders whether or not we can ever do anything significant in the face of adversity. We may wonder if we can do anything great or heroic. That is the power of story. It gives us the ability to take a story like Sam's and realize that we can make a difference. We see it happen, and it appears real for Sam, so we realize it can be real in our lives as well. Fairy tales and stories are far from useless; they tell us the truth about what can be in our world as well.

The triumph of returning to one's own hometown perhaps does not quite look like the ultimate victory over evil. It does not appear overly heroic. Watching the Ring fall into the fire seems like a much more appropriate climax. However, as Gandalf said, the entire reason that these hobbits, including the Ring-bearer, went on this journey was to prepare them to save their homeland. They did not save their homeland for all four of them though. Three of them were meant to go elsewhere. It was only saved for the hero of the story, Samwise Gamgee, who is the hero, not because of his great deeds, but rather because he was able to truly fulfill his purpose and fit into his place in the world. This helps ordinary people like you and I remember that our everyday lives can be heroic as well because we are right where we are meant to be.

Lava: A Story of Love and Hope

Carla Alvarez on the Deeper Themes within the Pixar Short

The world is looking for hope. We want to believe that whatever is going on, circumstances can change . . . things will get better. Pixar's 2015 short film, *Lava*, is based on the idea of hope that perseveres. Written and directed by James Ford Murphy, *Lava* tells the story of a volcano, alone in the sea, searching for love.

While the story could have been placed in any tropical island setting, its references are all Hawaiian. Murphy had always felt a special connection to the song *Somewhere Over the Rainbow* as performed by Israel Kamakawiwo'Ole, also known as the "Voice of Hawaii."[1] The inspiration

---

1 Renee Montagne, "Israel Kamakawiwo'ole: The Voice of Hawaii" (*NPR*, April 4, 2011), accessed December 1, 2015, http://www.npr.org/2010/12/06/131812500/israel-kamakawiwo-ole-the-voice-of-hawaii.

for *Lava* came to Murphy after visiting Hawaii on a family vacation. He was fascinated by the geological history of the Big Island, which is made up of five volcanoes that have joined together over time. He was particularly intrigued by a diorama of the island depicting "Lo'ihi," an underwater volcano that will, over time, join the other five volcanoes that make up the Big Island.[2]

The inspiration of the submerged volcano percolated together with his love for Hawaii for several years until his sister's wedding. Marrying for the first time at 43, he saw her joy in marrying her love that she had waited for for so long and it brought to his mind Lo'ihi, the submerged volcano waiting to be joined.[3] This was the seed of the song *Lava* and the short animated film based upon it.

In the opening scene of the film, we see a male volcano alone in the middle of the sea, surrounded by and supporting animal and marine life . . . all in pairs. He sees the love around him and begins his song reminiscent of the opening lines of Martin

---

[2] Lauren Davis, "The Real Geology Behind Pixar's Short Film *Lava*," accessed December 1, 2015, http://io9.com/the-real-geology-behind-pixars-short-film-lava-1713976956.

[3] "5 Questions with Disney/Pixar's *LAVA* director James Ford Murphy," (Khon2, November 3, 2014), accessed December 1, 2015, http://khon2.com/2014/11/03/5-questions-with-disneypixars-lava-director-james-ford-murphy/.

Luther King, Jr.'s famous speech as well as the lyrics of *Somewhere Over the Rainbow*:

> *I have a dream I hope will come true*
> *That you're here with me and I'm here with you*
> *I wish that the earth, sea, the sky up above-a*
> *Will send me someone to lava*

Time passes and he keeps singing, holding on to hope. With no evidence or sign that his words are being heard or that there is any point to his song at all, he keeps singing. As the Scriptures say, "Hope deferred makes the heart sick."[4] The volcano's deferred hope causes his lava to cool and harden until at last he is submerged beneath the sea. It seemed that his story was over and that his song was sung in vain.

Unbeknownst to the male volcano, his song is heard by a female volcano under the sea. She listens to and longs for his song, "knowing it was for her,"[5] until the time her lava erupts and she rises above the ocean surface . . . at just the moment he sinks behind her. Not seeing him and not knowing what has happened, she picks up his song where he left

---

[4] Proverbs 13:12.

[5] *Lava,* dir. by James Ford Murphy (Pixar Animation Studios, 2014).

off and begins to sing. When he hears her singing, his lava is built up again until he erupts above the sea and joins with her.

There are many parallels to the Christian faith. The male volcano had faith that just as all other creatures had a mate, that there must be one for him. As he saw goodness, love, and companionship in all and for all other things, there must be the same for him. He looked for something for which he had no evidence. There was no mate for him in site and he had never seen another of his type. The male volcano had, as the writer of Hebrew explains it, "the assurance of things hoped for, the conviction of things not seen."[6]

The volcano's faith in the coming of an unseen mate echoes God's instruction throughout the Old Testament to be "strong and courageous" and in the New to "stand firm." Even when there is no indication to believe otherwise, we are to hold on to the promises of God. In this seven minute film, there is no mention of God; however, the volcano had a belief that there is someone who could and would answer. Just as he was formed, that another like him could be as well.

---

[6] Hebrews 11:1.

Lava also illustrates 1 Corinthians 13:8 which states "love never fails." It could also be a parable with a picture of Hebrews chapter 10 to keep an unwavering hope in God who will be faithful (vs 23) and not to grow faint-hearted but to keep our confident hope (vs 35.) So strong was the volcano's belief in love and goodness that he continued singing his song to the very end.

But the most powerful illustration is that even when it seems all hope is gone, love wins through the faithfulness of God. The end of the volcano's story seemed to be one of disappointment, of unfulfilled hope. He believed and sang, but yet he sank alone. Whatever would come seemed to be too late. This is the picture of Abraham and Sarah who, although their bodies were as good as dead[7], they still believed God would fulfill his promise. It is the story of Esther and Mordecai who put their trust in God even when it seemed like there was no hope to turn the decree of Xerxes. It is the story of the resurrection, where life comes from death and victory from defeat. In each case it seemed the situation was beyond hope, that there was no way, but as with the story of the volcano, there was a

---

[7] Romans 4:19, Hebrews 11:12.

new beginning born from what seemed to be the end.

Watching the film for the first time, as the male volcano sank just as the one he was waiting for emerged, my Jewish friend said pessimistically, "That's just like life." When he emerged again to join his love I thought, "That's just like God."

THE POWER IN PAIN

Annie Nardone on the First-Hand Experience of Pain

May 2018,

I have been here before. This grief that crushes my soul like a black hole. I dream that I'm clawing at slippery, black walls as I slide farther down . . . to what? No bottom, because the grief is in layers, just like the layers of dark events of the past few months. Everything that has been impending is now concluding. Change plane reservations to NOW, not later, because hospice just called. She's in her final days . . . no, hours, they tell me. Tomorrow. Maybe. Or tonight.

Cancer has reared its ugly head in my family again. Dad's story ended in victory, so we know healing is possible. But how could this stupid disease come again, this time to my mother? Just one week ago we were in Minnesota, moving them into their new apartment, but now returned to

Virginia, I receive a call one day later from my dad to tell me "Mom has a tumor in her brain and it's big. I have to drive behind the ambulance to Rochester now." Dad, a quiet and capable man, sounds like a scared little boy. I'm calling their friends in Minnesota, trying to weave together a support system for him while he sits alone in a cold hospital waiting room, trying to absorb the idea that his wife of sixty years may die. A few hours later the surgeon calls, foregoing the time-consuming formality of permissions paperwork because "if they don't operate now, she's dead."

She makes it through surgery, but there are still traces of cancer. No matter, we've been here before with Dad. We'll win again. After all, there's the first great grandchild due in April! It's so easy to read God's purpose into something, isn't it? Surely, that baby will give mom hope and something to live for as she heals from surgery and endures radiation treatment.

Tonight, we meet the vet after hours to give him the kitten that my daughter has fed with a spoon and watered with a dropper hour-by-hour for days on end. We have to say goodbye, knowing that we are leaving him with the kindly vet, also knowing he's not going to be here when we return home. Pack our bags and all of our school work because we don't know when we will come home. Tumble out of the car at the airport in the middle of the night. **I feel hollow.** I read during the first flight because adrenaline and exhaustion prevent any rest. While we are running to catch our connecting flight, hospice calls. Mom slipped away peacefully at 6:30 a.m. Dad was with her, one arm in a cast and holding her hand with the other. We land in Minnesota with our sleep-deprived brains on autopilot. The vet calls. The kitten has died too.

Do we laugh at how ridiculous life seems at this point? I ask, "God, how is this a good idea?" I am overwhelmed. Drowning. Rapid-fire tragedy we cannot control, cannot fix, and certainly don't understand. I am numb and only reacting, fatigue so intense that my brain feels like I'm riding up in a sky-high elevator, just to plummet to the ground — over and over. I'm so dizzy and scattered, maybe I have a brain tumor too. Isn't that how it starts? No, now I'm being irrational; but nothing has made sense for months, so who knows.

My soul is imploding on itself, crumbling like a tower of cards, crushed.

It has to end. It doesn't end.

Death. And not just death of every sort, but the fallout from it all. The death of a parent and the disabling of the other in the same month; the death of my daughter's beloved kitten at the same time we are planning my mother's funeral; the death of a friendship. I am not unaccustomed to sorrow, but to see my children crawling through it and wanting to save them, help them, and cushion the blows that came at us from every direction all at once is overwhelming.

Years ago, I had read C.S. Lewis's book *A Grief Observed*, but only from the perspective of curiosity and admiration of his writing. Lewis married Joy Davidman, knowing that she had cancer. Her death, though not a complete surprise, moved him to a place beyond simple explanation. His teaching on pain and grief, examined and systematically explained in his prior apologetic writing *The Problem of Pain*, was turned upside down. Anguish became personal. Death is a different matter entirely when you are coping with the passing of *your own* spouse. And now I find myself in the middle of my own grief.

I realize that all along the road of mom's cancer, God was taking care of us, not by fixing the cancer, but by remaining steadfast in the midst of the storm. Like Lewis, I cried out, "Where is God?"[1] In *A Grief Observed*, he identifies this question as "one of

---

[1] C.S. Lewis, *A Grief Observed* (New York: HarperCollins, 1996) 5.

the most disquieting symptoms."[2] It is all well and good to tell me that suffering is a part of life; reading the account of someone who has actually faced the death of a loved one or a broken relationship is where I can find credibility and deeper understanding. Even when I couldn't see it in the moment, He cared for us from the periphery. Why is it so easy to forget that I have been here before? Joy's son, Douglas H. Gresham, wrote about this idea in the introduction to his stepfather's book *A Grief Observed*. We find ourselves back in the black hole of grief, but "what many of us discover in this outpouring of anguish is that we know exactly what [C.S. Lewis] is talking about. Those of us who have walked this same path, or are walking it as we read this book, find that we are not after all as alone as we thought."[3] God is faithful to place other people in our lives who understand our heartache and struggled through similar tragedy.

The Bible tells us that the night prior to his trial and crucifixion, Christ suffered deep anguish as he prayed in the garden of Gethsemane. Christ tells his disciples, "My soul is very sorrowful, even to death;

---

[2] Ibid.

[3] Ibid, xxxi.

remain here, and watch with me."[4] St. Luke describes Christ's torment, writing, "And being in agony he prayed more earnestly; and his sweat became like great drops of blood falling down to the ground."[5] The very Son of God agonized here on earth; He is no stranger to affliction, but understands the pain of mere mortals like C.S. Lewis, like you, and like me. He has gone before us; he has been there too. We can find assurance through example.

Standing in the airport and waiting for our connecting flight, the idea of Jesus's life comes to mind — not in an exceptionally theological moment, but more of a logical reset. Jesus was "a man of sorrows and acquainted with grief."[6] He knew bone-deep sorrow. What would earn me a pass from its grip if not even the Son of God was protected from it?

Then fragments of an old memory, another time and tragedy that left me nearly unable to breathe, come to my mind. I remember the times that I couldn't stand up — I could only hug my knees and scream for God to pay attention to my

---

[4] Matt. 26:38.

[5] Luke 22:44.

[6] Isaiah 53:3.

pleading. I demanded answers. I begged for them from a God who seemingly remained silent, watching me from some realm above. Like the grieving Lewis said, His silence felt like "a door slammed in your face."[7]

He finally answered my pleas, but on His terms and not mine. Two years would pass before I started to understand. He didn't rescue me out of the pain — He brought me through it . . . He can take the darkest suffering in our lives and turn it into something beautiful and useful. Now I use the experience of my pain and grief to minister to others who find themselves in circumstances that mirror mine. The difficult path that God helped me navigate became a map to guide others. Would we choose suffering? I doubt it. But look at what we would miss down the road if we chose the easy path — lessons learned that will in turn guide others. Suffering and sorrow led me to a deeper understanding of mercy and patience.

I have been here before. Even if this time it was trouble times three, I had the reminder that "Oh yes, I made it through." In *A Grief Observed*, we note that Lewis gradually turned in his view of grief through a process. He reacted with anger on the

---

[7] Lewis, *A Grief Observed*, xii.

first page of the book, writing with a rawness that is familiar to us. His realization, "No one ever told me that grief felt so like fear. I am not afraid, but the sensation is like being afraid,"[8] makes complete sense to me. That's it. Lewis nailed it. He told me to "keep on swallowing"[9] and that's the best I can do.

An accident or illness may suddenly take the life of someone we love and we are crushed in spirit. But the danger lies in swirling in our anger without moving on. Lewis wrestled with his anger toward God, but later there is a glimmer of recognition that he might have been too focused on demanding answers from God instead of being still. He considered that "I have gradually been coming to feel that the door is no longer shut and bolted. Was it my own frantic need that slammed it in my face? . . . Perhaps your own reiterated cries deafen you to the voice you hoped to hear."[10] Lewis shares his struggle with deep grief in a completely honest way. Christians often put on a mask that covers the real questions in their hearts. It is good to go to our God and ask those questions, just like Lewis shows us in *A Grief Observed.* Inevitably, we will be

---

[8] Ibid, 3.

[9] Ibid.

[10] Ibid., 46.

confronted with a grieving person who will not shy away from asking us, and if we have not been honest with ourselves and God about our own battles, we have little to offer. Lewis's book presents a timeless and compelling example of a deeply Christian man who needed answers and found resolution. Consider how many lives were changed by his bold and honest writing. His was and remains an example of a Christian whose imaginative and reasoned responses explain difficult topics like pain and tribulation.

Many of us have a grief story that leaves us bruised and bloodied. As difficult as it may be, we can use our experience to walk other people through their pain. I made it through the valley in no small part from the comfort I gleaned by reading Lewis's story. So often when we are in the midst of the mess we feel that no one else could possibly know our pain or ever survive what we are currently suffering. We must remind ourselves to open our eyes and acknowledge that what we learn to endure becomes the great lesson we share with others. That is why stories are so powerful. Through the retelling of our experience and the writing of other people, we discover that we are not alone. Whatever difficulty that you are in right now, someone else has been there and lived to tell the tale. There is strength, comfort, learning, and healing in shared stories.

> "Could Beethoven have written that glorious paean of praise in the "Ninth Symphony" if he had not had to endure the dark closing in of deafness? As I look through his work chronologically, there's no denying that it deepens and strengthens along with the deafness. Could Milton have seen all that he sees in *Paradise Lost* if he had not been blind? It is chastening to realize that those who have no physical flaw, who move through life in step with their peers, who are bright and beautiful, seldom become artists. The unending paradox is that we do learn through pain."

> —Madeline L'Engle, *Walking on Water*

COURAGE IN THE COSMOS

Daniel Ray on the Boldness of Our Story

"When physicists work on a theory, they are not dealing directly with nature," writes physicist Giovanni Vignale,

> . . . but with an abstract model which they have already decided which aspects of reality must be absolutely retained, and which ones can be dismissed. Often, in creating this model, they make bold and quite implausible assumptions, which can only be validated by the consistency of the results. But, to take such bold steps one cannot rely on calculation alone: it takes passion, imagination, a sense of beauty – all things that we grasp with our whole personality, and definitely with our heart.[1]

---

[1] Giovanni Vignale, *The Beautiful Invisible – Creativity, Imagination and Theoretical Physics* (Oxford: Oxford University Press, 2011), 3.

Through these bold and creative ventures, physicists have uncovered what seem like rather quixotic "rules" which govern the physical world we inhabit. For lack of a better term, most scientists call them "laws." And the laws that have been discovered strongly suggest we only have a few pieces of the puzzle. For every law we know of, there might be countless more waiting to be discovered. And what a marvel it is to those who first discover such laws, incredible and counterintuitive though they may first appear.

It took not a little courage for someone like Johannes Kepler to stand firm in his Protestant convictions in the midst of a great deal of counter-reformation turmoil. It also took not a little courage to publish his three laws of planetary motions early in the 17th century. For his new "laws" ran wholly counter to the centuries-old Aristotelian-Ptolemaic concepts of crystal spheres and the perfectly circular orbits of the planets. But when you wrestle with the god of war and all its irascible contrary motions as Kepler did and emerge victorious from the strife, you press on with a courage and boldness that only such trials can give.

Kepler's laws of planetary motion are now standard fare. But at the time they went against the grain of the accepted cosmological models. Planets don't move in perfect circles? What? The heavens are not "perfect"? How can this be? As it was the case when the Apostles first heard the story that their Teacher had risen from the dead. The story the women related to them "appeared to them as nonsense and they would not believe."[2] Not a very flattering account of the men who would soon become the foundational authority of the Church.

For the scientifically minded among us, though, the Resurrection is often said to be a *violation* of the laws of physics. Dead people simply do not come back to life. Entropy, right? You spill your tea and shatter your cup, but no battalion of the king's mounted troops can put all that back together again the way the teacup rested in your hands just moments before. Nothing can go against the ever-increasing entropic flow toward chaos. When you're dead, you're dead. The Apostles were just like us in this regard. Never had they considered the possibility of someone returning from the dead. And they spent some three years with Jesus. Of course the women's story would appear to them as nonsense. Even when Jesus showed Himself alive to

---

[2] Luke 24:11, NASB (and throughout).

people, Matthew records that some "worshiped *Him;* but some were doubtful."[3]

But can we finally say that the Resurrection of Jesus of Nazareth from the garden tomb is a *violation* of the laws of nature? Rather might it be in accordance with a greater reality, a deeper law, wholly unknown to our common sense? Kepler's ellipses, after all, certainly seemed to "violate" the allegedly known "laws" of crystal spheres and celestial perfection. The Resurrection may be a "bold and implausible assumption" to be sure, but it seems in the ever-increasing complexity and wonder that is regularly being discovered strongly suggests life and laws in the universe are stranger than anything we could imagine. The stuff of our everyday common experience is a great deal more uncommon than we ever have previously imagined. As theologian Leslie Newbigin puts it,

> It is obvious that the story of the empty tomb cannot be fitted into our contemporary worldview, or indeed into any worldview except one of which it is the starting point. That is, indeed, the whole point. What happened on that day is, according to the Christian tradition,

---

3 Matt. 28:17.

only to be understood by analogy with what happened on the day the cosmos came into being. It is a boundary event, at the point where (as cosmologists tell us) the laws of physics cease to apply. It is the beginning of a new creation – as mysterious to human reason as the creation itself.[4]

As the Apostle Paul exclaims, "Oh, the depth of the riches both of the wisdom and knowledge of God! How unsearchable are His judgments and unfathomable His ways!"

Consider[5] the phenomenally enigmatic star KIC 8462852, known more colloquially as Tabby's Star. It has been called the most mysterious star in the universe simply for the incredibly bizarre dimming of its light, as though some spectral apparition from the imagination of Edgar Allan Poe is repeatedly passing in front of it just to terrorize us. It might as well be a ghost, given all the other attempts at explanations that have been offered, including alien megastructures.[6] This stellar

---

[4] Leslie Newbigin, *The Gospel in a Pluralist Society* (Grand Rapids: Eerdmans, 1989), 11.

[5] Consider that *consider* means to "think with the stars" – *considereal*.

[6] Hannah Osbourne, "KIC 8462852: Alien Megastructure Star Starts Dimming Again—What Does It Mean?" *Newsweek*. Published May 26, 2017. Accessed March 2, 2018,

mystery is challenging every fiber of astrophysicists' understanding regarding the nature of stars. Astronomers have taken on a Hamlet-like interrogation of this celestial spirit,

> Angels and ministers of grace defend us!
>
> Be thou a spirit of health or goblin damn'd,
>
> Bring with thee airs from heaven or blasts from hell,
>
> Be thy intents wicked or charitable,
>
> Thou comest in such questionable shape
>
> That I will speak to thee: I'll call thee [Tabby's Star],
>
> King, father, royal Dane: O, answer me!

If human beings have their ultimate origin in the furnace of suns, as current conceptual models of our carbon suggest, then stars are our progenitors and Tabby's Star is a womb of nuclear wonder. Is it any wonder then that it occasionally goes dark? Is not that what happens in our light sometimes? Who knows? Do we ultimately come from the furnace of stars? That too seems rather disquieting. "O, answer me!" Is *that* really true?

---

http://www.newsweek.com/kic-8462852-alien-megastructure-dimming-astronomers-baffled-616346/.

Richard Burton, in his *Anatomy of Melancholy,* though writing a few hundred years before the advent of space telescopes, nonetheless captures the imaginative frenzy Tabby's Star has generated in the astronomical community. From giant alien megastructures to enormous Saturn-like planets, to comets, dust, what could it be?

> Methinks I hear, methinks I see
>
> Ghosts, goblins, fiends; my phantasy
>
> Presents a thousand ugly shapes,
>
> Headless bears, black men, and apes,
>
> Doleful outcries, and fearful sights,
>
> My sad and dismal soul affrights.
>
> All my griefs to this are jolly,
>
> None so damn'd as melancholy.[7]

Melancholy. It is the demented spectre that haunts human genius, a messenger of Satan sent to buffet and goad us toward the light. Its terrors often seem as though they will overwhelm us. We have not the requisite courage to face it many times. But what sort of light it is that gives our fainting hearts the courage to persevere. Like distant starlight that enlivens our sense of wonder,

---

[7] Richard Burton, *The Anatomy of Melancholy* (New York: New York Review Books, 2001), 12.

Jesus's light shines in the darkness of our melancholy. Even as Christians I think we often simply do not comprehend it. It startles us, even frightens us not a little. When Jesus first bodily appeared to some of His disciples, Luke records that "they were startled and frightened and thought that they were seeing a spirit."[8] But His appearing is not meant to keep us in bondage to fear, but to give us love and power and a sound mind.

Yet despite the gift of a sound mind, I still find myself not a little timid in discussing the Resurrection with skeptics, especially when their faces are already twisted up in expressions of incredulity and scorn.

In *Pride and Prejudice,* Jane Austen sums it up quite well. Through a brief exchange between Mr. Bennet and his young daughter Mary, I see myself all too well like Ms. Bennet and Mr. Bennet as a skeptical atheist looking for a loophole in my defenses.

> "What say you, Mary? For you are a young lady of deep reflection I know, and read great books, and make extracts."

---

[8] Luke 24:11.

Mary wished to say something very sensible, but knew not how.[9]

Yep.

That is indeed how I often feel as a Christian. What can I say? What should I say? Especially when the question is put to me by someone who already finds the idea of Jesus rising from the dead ridiculous! It knocks you a little speechless. There is finally nothing "sensible" about a man rising from the dead. Perhaps Christian apologetics has done the Resurrection a disservice in attempting to make it into a "reasonable" proposition when in reality, we should be reminding ourselves and others how shocking and out of this world it really is. The dimming and brightening of the bright and morning star (Rev. 22:16) ought to be a little disquieting to our common sense and make us all good physicists who are open to the shocking possibilities and uncommon oddities of the deeper laws of the universe; laws that leave us at times speechless. Proclamation of the universe's greatest wonder of all, the resurrection of the Lord Jesus, requires boldness and courageousness that is finally not our own.

---

[9] Jane Austen, *Pride and Prejudice*, Project Gutenberg, March 10, 2018, accessed September 3, 2018, http://www.gutenberg.org/files/1342/1342-h/1342-h.htm.

"And they went out and fled from the tomb, for trembling and astonishment had gripped them; and they said nothing to anyone, for they were afraid."[10]

---

[10] Mark 16:8.

The Homeric Versus the Christian Ideal of Man

Josiah Peterson on Contrasting the Nature of Humanity

As Western culture becomes more and more post-Christian, it will unsurprisingly bear more and more resemblance to its pre-Christian roots. One of the dominant cultural forces shaping the classical Greek worldview was Homer's epics poems. Homer envisions a cosmos conceived from chaos where order is an aberration rather than the norm.[1] Anthropomorphic and capricious Greek gods are amoral and the prospects of the afterlife are

---

[1] Holly Ordway, "Plato and Aristotle," (lecture, APOL 5330: Houston Baptist University, 2018).

dismal.[2] In such a chaotic world – not far from the world envisioned by many a modern philosopher – the ideal man is one who is strong enough and smart enough to survive and get what he wants. This ideal is manifested throughout Homer's epic poem, *The Odyssey,* in the character Odysseus who uses his strength and cunning to survive his tumultuous journey home and enact vengeance upon the suitors who have been wooing his wife and plaguing his household in his absence. This Homeric ideal of man as self-serving survivor stands in stark contrast to the Christian ideal of man, the God-man Jesus Christ, who forgoes worldly comfort and lays down his life for others.

Homer was the poet of pagan antiquity whose narrative depictions of the Trojan War and the return of the Achaian warriors, particularly Odysseus, most shaped the education and worldview of the ancient Greeks. It is primarily Homer whom Plato attacks in the *Republic* in his diatribe against the corruptions of poetry.[3] Mythology's influence was ubiquitous in the art,

---

[2] Holly Ordway, "Greek Myth," (lecture, APOL 5330: Houston Baptist University, 2018).

[3] Plato, *Republic*, translated by Robin Waterfield (New York: Oxford World's Classics, 2008), 72-93.

architecture, and ceremony of Greek life and provided the underlying narrative shaping the philosophical and moral imaginations of the Greek people who grew up on these stories. In the absence of systematic philosophy and ethics, Homer's myths provided the Greeks an imaginative conception of the way the world works and a model for human behavior. Plato was not wrong to think the influence of myths of grave importance for society.

Of the myriad heroes Homer eulogizes, Odysseus receives the most attention, featuring prominently in both *The Iliad* and *The Odyssey*. In the former, the cunning Odysseus is preferred over the brave and powerful Ajax to be the recipient of Achilles's armor, an incident which Thomas Bulfinch interprets as the Greeks "placing wisdom before valour."[4] As the narrative heir of Achilles, Odysseus is a more relatable hero than the nearly invulnerable demigod he succeeds. Odysseus outlasts the stronger Achilles and Ajax through his cunning and determination, and it is ultimately Odysseus's plan of the Trojan Horse that leads to the capture of Troy and his epithet, "sacker of

---

[4] Thomas Bulfinch, *Mythology* (New York: Random House, 1934), 184.

cities." Odysseus is one of only a handful of Achaian heroes to make it home during the perilous *Nostoi*, or return from Troy, and this tale makes up the bulk of the narrative of Homer's *Odyssey*.[5]

Odysseus's homeward journey through monster-infested seas under the wrath of vengeful gods reveals the chaotic nature of the mythological cosmos. Sea voyages are not just unpredictable due to weather, but also due to islands inhabited by cyclopes, enchantresses, and six-headed monsters. Some of these trials are unavoidable, as in the case of Scylla and Charybdis which must be passed through for Odysseus to return home. But in many cases, "there is no good reason for his torment," observes John Mark Reynolds. "It is simply the will of the gods and the bad fortune of Odysseus."[6] Homer's *Odyssey* thus suggests a pessimistic view of the world. Holly Ordway observes that "fundamentally, the world as the pagan Greeks saw it was chaotic, unpredictable, and dangerous."[7] From this we are able to infer a broader

---

[5] Homer, *The Odyssey*, translated by Richard Lattimore (New York: Harper, 2007), 4.

[6] John Mark Reynolds, *When Athens Met Jerusalem* (Downers Grove, IL: IVP Academic, 2009), 26.

[7] Holly Ordway, "Greek Myth," (lecture, APOL 5330: Houston Baptist University, 2018).

cosmological structure for Greek society in which chaos is the essential feature of the universe and against which nomos, or conventional society, is the fragile effort of men just trying to get by.[8] The idea of a *logos*, or non-contingent order and reason, was still centuries away for the ancient Greeks.

The opening of the *Odyssey* presents a tale of death and discord, commensurate with the chaotic cosmos. After a brief invocation to the muses noting Odysseus's troubled homecoming, the scene shifts to a council of the Olympian gods. The gods lament the death of Agamemnon, whose murder by his wife's lover upon his return from Troy the gods had failed to prevent. The absence of Poseidon from the council allows Athena to make a petition on behalf of Odysseus, whom Poseidon hates for having killed his son Polyphemus. Zeus favors Athena's plea and dispatches Hermes to direct the nymph Calypso to release Odysseus, whom she has been keeping prisoner. This opening scene reveals that gods cannot provide a stable foundation for the Greek cosmos since they are not all powerful and their wills are not united. As Ordway succinctly observes, "None of them are the creator

---

[8] Holly Ordway, "Plato and Aristotle," (lecture, APOL 5330: Houston Baptist University, 2018).

of the cosmos; none of them are all powerful or all wise, certainly none of them are all good."[9]

Homer's depiction of Hades, the realm of the dead, offers no more accountability or consolation than do the gods for the troubled soul. It is a realm of shades. Reynolds describes Odysseus's visit to the underworld as revealing the "hopeless fate of the human dead," in which "all the fame won in the Trojan War means nothing in the face of death."[10] The shade of Achilles describes the land of the dead as a place "where the senseless dead men dwell, mere imitations of perished mortals."[11] When Odysseus tries to encourage Achilles, saying, "and now in this place you have great authority over the dead," Achilles replies, "O shining Odysseus, never try to console me for dying. I would rather follow the plow as a thrall to another man, one with no land allotted him and not much to live on, than be a king over all the perished dead."[12] If even the greatest among the dead lament their plight, and the most celebrated of worldly accomplishments

---

[9] Holly Ordway, "Greek Myth," (lecture, APOL 5330: Houston Baptist University, 2018).

[10] Reynolds, 26-27.

[11] Homer, 180.

[12] Homer, 180.

make no difference to one's eternal fate, then the afterlife can serve little purpose for directing men's lives beyond driving them to avoid death as long as possible. Plato will later condemn Achilles's statement for making men craven, valuing life more than honor or duty.[13]

Within this pessimistic worldview, with no hope or direction from above or below, Homer sets forth an ideal of man that puts a premium on survival skills – particularly strength, cunning, and determination – to the exclusion of objective moral principles. Richard Martin observes, "Most striking to modern sensibilities is the idea that [Homer's] heroes are not necessarily morally upright . . . Odysseus can bring about the deaths of many, intentionally, without remorse, and still be considered a model of toughness, skill, or endurance."[14] These laudable qualities are highlighted in the many epithets given to Odysseus throughout Homer's poems. He is described as strong: godlike, great, foreman of men, hardy, famous spearman, great seasoned old campaigner, sacker of cities. He is cunning, of many designs,

---

[13] Plato, 80.

[14] Richard Martin, "Introduction," *The Iliad of Homer*, translated by Richard Lattimore, (Chicago: University of Chicago Press, 2011), 26.

crafty, a man for all occasions, a man skilled in all ways of contending, a man like Zeus himself for council, man of many resources, nimble-witted, wise, and resourceful. He is determined, much-enduring, stalwart, man of many sorrows, man of many ways, the wanderer. The epithets that come closest to having moral content are noble, gallant, and "great glory of the Achaians," but these are primarily applied with reference to Odysseus's strength, courage, and cunning during the Trojan War.

While most of his epithets focus on his cunning, Odysseus's cunning would be insufficient without the strength to survive in the rough and tumble Homeric world. Shipwrecked by Poseidon's wrath, Odysseus is tempest-tossed for days before he is able to swim to the shore of the Phaiakians' land. Back in Ithaka, it is Odysseus's strength as well as his stratagem that enables him to best the suitors in the shooting contest and the battle that follows. Homer makes a point of highlighting how Odysseus is the only one able to string the bow and complete the shooting contest, clearly establishing his hero's physical superiority over his rivals.

While physical strength is a prerequisite, it is not sufficient on its own for survival and ingenuity must step in where strength and courage fail.[15] This is particularly shown in the incident with the cyclops, Polyphemus. It is Odysseus's hubris that gets him and many of his men caught in the cave of the giant in the first place, but it is Odysseus's cunning that gets any of them out alive. Odysseus restrains the men from attacking the cyclops in his sleep, recognizing that without him they have no way of moving the boulder from the entrance of the cave. They determine instead to blind the cyclops and escape on the underbellies of his sheep as they go out to pasture. Odysseus adds the extra ploy of telling Polyphemus that his name is "Nobody," so that when Polyphemus calls for help, he will not receive any.

Determination is the final quality required to survive in the world of Greek myths. Several times Odysseus might have yielded to death – from despair at having been blown back from sight of home when his men opened the bag of winds, from the despair of floating on flotsam after his raft is wrecked by Poseidon, or from capitulating to the desires of Calypso or Circe and staying with the goddesses rather than to return home.[16] His iron

---

[15] Ibid, 8-9.

[16] It is true that in leaving the goddesses' islands Odysseus forgoes a kind of immortality. This could be read as Odysseus's

will is on proud display throughout the story and would not have been missed by attentive audiences.

While survival is of great importance for the Homeric hero, the next greatest thing is to be able to accomplish one's desires for fame and fortune. Homer makes it a point to emphasize that after leaving Troy, Odysseus and his men raid an innocent village on their way home. Homer also highlights that the gifts of the Phaiakians are more valuable than what Odysseus might have brought back from Troy. Telemachus is sent on his own journey in order to win fame and bring home gifts. Odysseus is not satisfied to remain in obscurity on an island with a goddess as her plaything. He wants to return to his land and kingship, living in comparative fame and fortune to those around him.

It should not be surprising that such amoral acquisitiveness is part of the Greek ideal when their gods display the same characteristics. To quote Ordway, "As depicted in the stories, the gods were not moral beings; they were not fundamentally

---

hubris getting in the way of his survival or simply that Odysseus sees living in obscurity as a slave to a goddess as little different from the afterlife he is trying to avoid.

interested in your good; and the myths are full of stories of mortal women being raped by Zeus or transformed or killed in horrible ways by other gods and goddesses for no good reason."[17] If neither the gods nor the afterlife offer any kind of accountability, men's actions should be to maximize their personal gains while they can. Any piety involved is usually just as self-serving.

Moral values are not compelling in the *Odyssey*. Compassion is casually dismissed with the passing description of Odysseus raiding the Kikonians on his return from Troy: "I sacked their city and killed their people, and out of their city taking their wives and many possessions we shared them out."[18] The only remorse from this occasion is that they did not leave swiftly enough to escape reprisal. Additionally, there is the praise lavished on Autolykos, Odysseus's "noble" grandfather-in-law, who "surpassed all men in thievery and the art of the oath [perjury]" and who was favored by the god Hermes for all his sacrifices.[19] Faithfulness is admired but more as a praise of iron will than from

---

[17] Holly Ordway, "Greek Myth," (lecture, APOL 5330: Houston Baptist University, 2018).

18 Homer, 138.

19 Ibid., 292.

moral purpose. Odysseus is praised for being enduring and steadfast on his quest to return home, but he happily sleeps with the goddesses he meets along the way, including after he his release from Calypso has been announced. Even Odysseus's tragic flaw of hubris, which gets him into trouble with the cyclops when Odysseus waits in the cave in against his men's urging and when he shouts back his name as they are making their escape, is condemned more for its adverse survival value than for anything inherently wrong with pride. In this case, cunning is partly able to compensate for hubris as Odysseus is able to trick the cyclops and make his escape on the underbellies of the monster's sheep. Physical or intellectual strength can, at least in part, make up for moral failings.

The Christian ideal of man is shaped by a very different foundational story, that of creation, fall, and redemption and the saving work of Jesus Christ. Christianity holds that an all-powerful God created the universe and that the original design for world and man was good. God gave man free will so that His creatures could be more like Him. When his creatures fell into sin, God did not turn his back on them but rather sent his Son, Jesus, to be born amongst men, live a perfect life, and die as a sacrifice to atone for the sins of all mankind.

Because of Christ's redeeming work, man can live forever in glory with God after they die. In the Christian worldview, Jesus is the ideal man. Christians are called to be like Christ and to take up their cross and follow Him in humility and service of others.

Jesus displays many of the same qualities as Odysseus but directs them toward radically different ends. While Jesus is strong – capable of raising the dead and calming the sea, besides chasing out merchants from the temple with a whip – he is meek, letting little children sit on his lap. While Jesus is crafty enough to best the Pharisees and even Satan himself in arguments, he uses his discernment to ask the questions and give the answers that his thirsty audience needs to hear. Jesus's determined will takes him to death, not away from it. And while Jesus "thought it not robbery to be equal with God," he condescended to take the role of a servant in the likeness of men, humbling himself and becoming "obedient unto death, even the death of the Cross."[20] It is true that God subsequently exalts Jesus and He receives praise from the people of the world, but the process involved the most humiliating and painful

---

[20] Philippians 2: 6-9 (KJV)

suffering that could be imagined: the fellowship of the godhead broken while Jesus descended into Hell before his resurrection on the third day.

It should be no surprise that Homeric mythology and Christianity share similar ideal qualities for only good qualities can make someone capable of accomplishing anything. Who can imagine a world in which weakness, foolishness, and spinelessness are exalted? But it should equally be no surprise that the differences in the cosmology, theology, and teleology of the two worldviews leads to radically different founding narratives. One believes in grabbing what one can in an ultimately futile fight against chaos, while the other holds confidently to an inevitable victory of the logos over the chaos and all that yielded themselves to it.

Relict

Karise Gililland on the Transition from
Bewildered Suffering to Active Hope

Flying all to pieces, you
vanished
One brilliant flaming mass,
flitting off in a million wingbeats
and the stopping of my heart
shaken from your roost
the trembling in the trees,
the rattle to the very roots
sent you scattered.

Bewitched, a heinous game of hide- and- seek
transitory glance
of wing, a flash of orange, and then
you were off and flew away again
Miles away, the trees
snatched you from all sight,
cryptic keepsafe.

Straying, your wings would freeze
(delicate, trembling things)
 certain degrees allow the allopatric;
 survival's separation
mimics a mountain keep-
The price paid for that safety
is steep; far countries cost.

I lay a garden on the hearth
all your favorite flowers,
sunny minutes stacked in hours,
the snow outside outwits at every turn.
Daneus, perplexed.
Waiting for you
to migrate back to me
is double winter
Will all those so fractured find the way back
home?

I know for whom I watch,
 dissolved through distance.

In a chance, a laugh, a moment
You have landed on my shoulder, flown in
fleetingly
Shyly for second, searching.

Sometimes I think all of you will come back to me,

Flying back in mass of glory

And shake of golden sun

Surrounded in the garden by the spicy scent of roses;

spell undone.

A 'relict' is "a remnant of a formerly widespread species that persists in an isolated area."[1] This poem is dedicated to those who've watched someone they love disappear and fly away into a million pieces. Perhaps they were not the same because of illness of mind or body, spiritual wanderings, rebellion, death. Perhaps you get them back as I have, in pieces, in fleeting glances or expressions, a relict of a smile- but only for a short while, and then they're gone again. Sometimes, we long for the whole person we were before a crisis, before illness, or depression. We wonder if we will even return to our whole, healed selves.

Like the life cycle of the migratory Monarch butterfly, this suffering and symbolic resurrection demonstrates repeated regeneration: life, changes, seeming death, transformation, and shivers of

---

[1] https://www.merriam-webster.com/dictionary/relict

hope. The irregular rhythm of this poem reflects the same sort of transition from bewildered suffering to active, poignant hope.

We long for that ultimate healing, when "everything broken is made new again" and the spell is utterly undone.

The Making of a Hero

Carla Alvarez on the Changing Modern
Perspective of Heroism

Courage comes in many forms. There is the courage of the moment when an individual rises to a challenge. There is the courage that is found in a group, a banding together and facing the odds. However, there is another sort of courage that begins in defeated circumstances with a person whom one would never pick to overcome. It is a courage that begins with a building of bravery and a turning of timidity to tenacity. It is a reforming, and because this transformation takes place not in a moment but through a painful step by painful step journey, one challenge overcome at a time; this is the type of courage that endures.

Courage is denoted by action. There must be something within that impels the action. As Lewis notes in his review on Ajax and Greek Tragedy, "behaviour is primarily a symptom from which to infer the 'haunting' latencies of the psyche."[1] It must be within first before it can come out.

This has not always been our belief or how our stories have been told. In the ancient myths, heroes were those who were of divine descent. They could perform extraordinary feats because they themselves were extraordinary, more than human. In the same essay, Lewis points out this change in origin of the impetus came about because of "Christianity and then by liberal individualism."[2] Our stories of courage shifted from the divinely gifted few among the ordinary masses to the Everyman: stories where the innate human dignity flowers and flourishes. The extension of this is that the courageous and benevolent acts of the hero displace the demigods from the pedestal they formerly occupied.

Culture Needs Heroes

A culture is shaped by the heroes that it reveres. A culture's stories portray heroes with qualities

---

[1] C.S. Lewis, "Ajax and Others: John Jones, On Aristotle and Other Greek Tragedy," in *Image and Imagination* (New York, NY: Cambridge University Press, 2013), 192.

[2] Ibid.

that the society values and which citizens should emulate. However, there is an interesting shift that has occurred in the past several decades in the popular stories of our culture. As our society has progressed into postmodernism and further away from Christian values, so have our heroes. Our heroes are no longer those who exemplify praiseworthy character qualities such as goodness, fidelity, and kindness, but there is almost a glorification of the very opposite. As Louis Markos notes in *Restoring Beauty*, "We are often more afraid of beauty than of ugliness.[3]"

Not only is the ugly and the vile celebrated, but along with this has come the devaluation of the self, the intrinsic worth of the individual. Our heroes don't look like us anymore. Luke of *Star Wars* is born with an innate ability to manipulate the Force: part of a class of a sci-fi version of demigods, if you will. We have returned to a stratification in the cosmos of cultural heroes found among that of the ancient pagans, sometimes with literal reintroductions into popular culture of ancient gods such as Thor and Loki.

---

[3] Louis Markos, *Restoring Beauty: The Good, The True, and The Beautiful in the Writings of C.S. Lewis* (Colorado Springs, CO: Biblical Publishing, 2010).

What encouragement can the common man draw from the exploits of these super beings? Example cannot be taken from them as they are in another class entirely. The only message that can be taken is to wait for someone better equipped to handle the problems life brings. Passivity is cultivated. A spotlight on this dilemma is made in this year's release, *The Incredibles 2*. The sister (and villain) of the superhero patron wants to destroy the supernaturally gifted because she resents the public's reliance upon them and blames this reliance for her parents' death.[4] As Richard Brody points out in his review of the movie in *The New Yorker*, the film director Brad Bird presents both the reliance on these super beings as well as the super heroes' "detachment . . . from morality" as a good and desirable thing.[5] The message is that there is one set of rules for the small group of gifted and another for everyone else. In this worldview the gifted, who can be identified as those Lewis labeled the "Conditioners" in *The Abolition of Man*, have the

---

[4] Brad Bird, *The Incredibles 2* (Pixar Animation Studios, 2018).

[5] Richard Brody, "Review: The Authoritarian Populism of 'Incredibles 2,'" *The New Yorker*, June 19, 2018, accessed August 30, 2018, https://www.newyorker.com/culture/richard-brody/review-the-authoritarian-populism-of-incredibles-2.

right to decide the course of action and the destiny of all others.[6]

So what is the answer? If we are to reclaim our culture and reinstate the value and potential for greatness that is found in each human being rather than the dependence of the masses on the preternaturally gifted few, what kinds of stories should be told?

The Stories that Need to be Told

In a culture that is searching for meaning, it is more important than ever to tell stories that point to the path of courage for each individual. As Markos quotes from *The Sacred Romance,* that "In some deep place within, we remember what we were made to be, we carry with us the memory of gods, image-bearers walking in the Garden."[7] Not a

---

[6] C. S. Lewis, *The Abolition of Man* (New York, NY: HarperCollins, 2001). 60-61. "But the man-moulders of the new age will be armed with the powers of an omnipotent state and an irresistable scientific technique: we shall get at last a race of conditioners who can really cut out all posterity in what shape they please . . . It is the function of Conditioners to control, not obey them [objective values]. They know how to *produce* conscience and decide what kind of conscience they will produce."

[7] Markos. 10. Markos quotes from Chapter 7 of *The Sacred Romans* by Brent Curtis and John Eldredge. The full quote: "Every woman is in some way searching for or running from her beauty and every man is looking for or avoiding his strength. Why? In some deep place within, we remember what we were made to be, we carry with us the memory of gods, image-bearers walking in the Garden. So why do we flee our essence? As hard it may be for us to see our sin, it is far

separate class of demigods, but rather we are called to be the children of God. We matter.

However this path has obstacles of our own making: our pride, our flaws, and our failures. We look to our past and circumstances which often seem overwhelming; it looks as if we will never overcome. When we cannot see beyond our present circumstances and the way to a different outcome, it is hard to have hope. The stories of personal transformation, showing how one person went from a failure to victor can encourage those looking for an answer. As Nicole Howe notes in her essay on Augustine's *Confessions*, "the journey of wandering and overcoming is not a physical journey; it is a spiritual one."[8] The stories of true value are not just those with quirky characters and interesting plot twists, but those that illustrate the path of personal transformation and growth.

An example of this type can be seen in two very different stories in two different mediums: the

---

harder still for us to remember our glory. The pain of the memory of our former glory is so excruciating, we woudl rather stay in the pigsty than return to our true home."

[8] Nicole Howe, "Augustine's *The Confessions*: The Power of Spiritual Autobiography," *An Unexpected Journal* 1, no. 2 (Summer 2018):87.

book *Till We Have Faces* by C.S. Lewis,[9] and the film *Dear Frankie* (2004) directed by Shona Auerbach.[10] Each story begins with a conflicted female protagonist who hides from the truth in one way or another. Both rise above an abusive background. Both begin with a distorted view of love and operate out of fear. The themes of the two stories are similar; however, the details are very different.

Till We Have Faces is Lewis's retelling of the myth of Psyche and Cupid. Set in the fictional kingdom of Glome (a distant neighbor of Greece), the story is told from the perspective of Psyche's sister, Orual. From birth, Psyche is beautiful both in word and in deed. The outer beauty is a manifestation of the inner grace. Orual describes it as:

> It was a beauty that did not astonish you till afterwards when you had gone out of sight of her and reflected on it. While she was with you, you were not astonished. It seemed the most natural thing in the world as the Fox delighted to say, "She was according to nature"; what every woman, even every thing ought to have

---

[9] C.S. Lewis, *Till We Have Faces: A Myth Retold* (New York, NY: Harcourt, Inc., 1956).

[10] Shona Auerbach, *Dear Frankie* (Miramax, 2004).

been and meant to be, but had missed by some trip of chance. Indeed when you looked at her you believed for a moment, that they had not missed it. She made beauty all around her.[11]

Orual, on the other hand was singularly ugly. She did not draw all people to her through face and form, but she cared for Psyche after her mother's death. Psyche was the focal point in her life. When Psyche was offered to the Shadow brute to appease the anger of Aphrodite (known as Ungual in Glome), she risked the wrath of the king and the people in an attempt to save her.

However Orual, as did the sister in the original myth, pushed Psyche to disobey her love's command by looking upon him, precipitating a disastrous series of events. Psyche was then lost to her and Orual had to continue her life alone. This love that had been the focal point of her life turned into bitterness: bitterness against the gods and bitterness against Psyche herself. For her love for Psyche was, as Lewis refers to it in *The Four Loves* a "Need-love,"[12] one which loves because of what it

---

[11] Ibid. 22.

[12] C.S. Lewis, "The Four Loves," in *The Family Christian Library: The Beloved Works of C.S. Lewis* (Grand Rapids, MI: Family Christian Press, 1960), 211–288.

receives in that love. It was, as Orual's mentor Fox warned her, "one part love in your heart, and five parts anger, and seven parts pride."[13]

This "Need-love," because it is based in self, does not end simply in being filled by the object of its affection, it must devour. As Psyche told Orual,

> You are indeed teaching me about kinds of love I did not know. It is like looking into a deep pit. I am not sure whether I like your kind better than hatred. Oh, Orual—to take my love for you, because you know it goes down to my very roots and cannot be diminished by any other newer love, and then to make of it a tool, a weapon, a thing of policy and master, an instrument of torture—I begin to think I never knew you.[14]

This theme of a corrupted and manipulative love, a "Need-love," is also found in the film *Dear Frankie*. The protagonist is a mother who is on the run from her abusive husband with her son and her mother. As with Orual's possessive love towards Psyche, the husband's love had long ago devolved into a thing that damaged and devoured.

---

[13] Lewis, *Till We Have Faces*. 148.

[14] Ibid. 165.

Directed by Shona Auerbach, the film illustrates a woman transformed over the course of the film, from one who lives in fear to a lioness who faces it.[15] However, this change comes gradually, slowly building like the beautiful melody of the theme song composed by Alex Heffes. We may not be able to put our finger exactly on the moment when the change occurs, but the full transformation is evident when the moment of truth comes.

When we meet Lizzie and her son, Frankie, she is arriving at a new town to temporarily call home. In contrast to Psyche who traveled the land to perform quests to be reunited to her love, Lizzie goes to great lengths to stay out of her husband's reach. For three years she has moved from town to town in Scotland, always on guard, ready to pack up and leave at a moment's notice. She lives like a refugee escaping the terror of her former life, always trying to stay one step ahead of her past which is trying to catch up with her.

In her effort to protect Frankie from the knowledge of what his father is and to keep questions at bay, she fabricates a story that his father is a seaman on a ship called Accra. In order to continue this charade, she writes periodic letters to

---

[15] Shona Auerbach, *Dear Frankie* (Miramax, 2004).

Frankie impersonating his father as he should be and with which Frankie corresponds. This deception is motivated by love and a desire to keep her son safe; however, like Orual's, it is a controlling love. Just as Orual withhholds bits of information in order to manipulate outcomes, such as acknowledging she did actually catch a glimpse of Psyche's home when speaking to Fox and distorting Fox's words when convincing Psyche to break her word to her husband, Lizzie keeps tight control on the information she shares with those around her. It is this manipulation of truth that brings about a crisis that forces a revelation in the end. [16] [17]

Development Through Circumstance

However, before the shadow can lift, darkness has to be exposed to the light . . . especially the darkness within. Orual loses the person closest to her by trying to control and refusing to let go. In her mind, she is in the right of it and her actions are justified. As with the superheroes in *The Incredibles 2*, she sets her own rules. Refusing to reflect on her own actions after the loss of Psyche, she continues

---

[16] Lewis, *Till We Have Faces*, 133-134.

[17] Ibid, 161.

on to rule the kingdom of Glome in service of others, but always alone.

If Orual's "Need-love" was a combination of love, anger, and pride, Lizzie's is equal parts fear and love. She keeps her secrets from everyone around her . . . her son, her mother, and her friends who are by necessity transitory . . . in an effort to maintain control of the situation. However, for Lizzie, circumstances begin to escalate that are far beyond her control.

After the little family begins to get established in their new community and obtains a sense of balance, exposure threatens on two different fronts. The first comes in the form of Frankie's cocky friend Ricky who shows him a newspaper announcement that the ship Accra will be docking in Greenock the following week, making a bet with Frankie that his dad will not come to see him. Betting his prized cards against Frankie's precious stamp collection, he seems certain that Frankie's father will be a no-show. From where does this confidence come? Perhaps Auerbach agrees with filmmaker Krzystof Kieslowski who once stated, "Children know more because they think with their instinct, not their reason."[18] Somehow Ricky senses the situation is off and believes he has a sure thing.

This revelation also prompts a second issue not immediately apparent. Because Frankie diligently charts the path of his dad's ship, his map shows the ship should be approaching the coast of Africa, not anywhere near Greenock, Scotland. This begins to raise questions in Frankie's own mind which are pieced together in the end. Lizzie, like Orual and Lewis's "Conditioners", believes she has the best in mind for her son; however, within each of us is a desire for truth that will forever push against the curtain of deception, no matter how lovingly hung.

However, it is not only this incident and the pending exposure to Frankie that is disturbing Lizzie's world. Her past life is also threatening to catch up with her. Lizzie's mother, Nell, discovers an ad looking for Lizzie and Frankie placed by Lizzie's in-laws. Nell attempts to get her son-in-law's family to leave them alone, but instead the size of the ad is exponentially increased along with a photo of Lizzie. The family, like Ricky, is not going to go away quietly.

---

[18] Simon Hattenstone, "Krzysztof Kieslowski Interviewed for Three Colours Red," *The Guardian*, November 8, 1994, accessed December 1, 2015, http://www.theguardian.com/film/2011/nov/09/krzysztof-kieslowski-interview.

Exposing Darkness to Light

These incidents occurring all at one time make Lizzie realize that she cannot continue the deceit. She begins to tell Frankie; however, when she realizes how emotionally invested he is in the imaginary picture of his father she has created, she is spurred to drastic and ill-considered action. Rather than confessing the whole, she instead decides to find a man, a stranger, who will impersonate Frankie's father for one day. After failing miserably at the local pub, she is disconsolate and wanders the streets ending up by the bay. It is here that her friend, Marie, finds her the next morning. The entire sequence is mostly silent. It is the silence itself that conveys Lizzie's loneliness and desperation. Lizzie confesses her plight and Marie offers to find a man to fit the job, a stranger to play Frankie's dad for a single day. This releasing of her tightly controlled secret to another is the beginning of Lizzie's transformation. As she acknowledges her vulnerability and opens up to another, the chains of manipulation, control, and fear begin to loose their hold.

While circumstances cumulate quickly in Lizzie's life, Orual's transformation from one consumed by a "Need-love" to surrendering to the

Divine "Gift love" takes place over a longer period of time.[19] Although no one takes the place that Psyche held in her heart, through the years there are others close to her which are impacted by her self-focused love: Fox, her mentor; Bardia, her second-in-command; and Redieval, her remaining sister. Because her opinion and view of the people close to her is defined by the actions and attention coming in to her, how her own needs are filled, not only does she never truly see them, but she herself is never truly known because her "glass," to use the Apostle Paul's metaphor, is clouded with self-interest.[20]

Even the love and care poured into Psyche was tainted with need, Psyche may have been loved and admired by all, but Orual was loved by Psyche. If all admire a desired one but the desired one admires you, you are in the superior position. From the first, Orual's care is motivated by a desire to control, it is a selfish and jealous love as finally revealed in the conclusion when she confronts the gods to make her complaint for their actions.

---

[20] 1 Corinthians 13:12. KJV. "For now we see through a glass, darkly; but then face to face: now I know in part; but then I shall know even as also I am known.

We want to be our own. I was my own and Psyche was mine and no one else had any other right to her. Oh you'll say you took her away into bliss and joy such as I could never have given her, and I ought to have been glad of it for her sake. Why? What should I care for some horrible, new happiness which I hadn't given her and which separated her from me? Do you think I wanted her to be happy, that way? It would have been better if I'd seen the Brute tear her in pieces before my eyes.[21]

Death Before Rebirth

For both Lizzie and Orual, before there can be a rebirth into something new, that which is corrupted in the old must die. Lizzie must rise above the fear which has bound her and Orual must release the pride which has prevented her from seeing the truth of her actions. For both, the spiritual renewal is precipitated by a physical death.

While there have been outbursts where Orual's self-centered actions are on display throughout the narrative, the only perspective given to the reader is Orual's own. In her mind, her actions are

---

[21] C.S. Lewis, *Till We Have Faces,* 291-292.

warranted. It is not until the death of her close friend and military commander, Bardia, that she is forced to examine herself. Throughout his final illness, Orual is indignant that he is away for so long, certain that it is his wife that is keeping him away. Even when she hears of his death, her only thoughts are of how it affects her and regrets that "all would be bearable if, only once, I could have gone to him and whispered in his ear, 'Bardia, I loved you."[22]

It is not until she visits Bardia's widow, Ansit, to give her condolences that Orual is forced to take a hard look at herself, her actions, and her motivations. Pushed past courtesy in her grief, Ansit confronts Orual with her narcissism which consumed without thought of those around her. The clear mirror held by Bardia's wife is not one Orual can ignore.

Orual leaves incensed, but it is no use. Her conscience so long muffled is revived and "those divine Surgeons had me tied down and were at work. My anger protected me only for a short time; anger wearies itself out and truth comes in. For it was all true - truer than Ansit could know."[23] A

---

[22] Ibid, 258.

[23] Ibid, 266.

flood of other memories come in until Orual has to admit that what she had called love is "a sickening thing."[24] All that she had prided herself on is as ashes until "nearly all that I called myself went with it. It was if my whole soul had been one tooth and now that tooth was drawn. I was a gap. And now I thought I had come to the very bottom that the gods could tell me no worse.[25]"

For Lizzie, it is the impending death of her estranged husband that causes her to face her fears. The film up to this point has been one of sparse words and stretches of silence. Meaning is communicated through what is not said. In contrast, the hospital scene where she faces her husband is the most verbal and sound filled portion of the film. It is as if Lizzie steps from the half-light of a twilight world back into reality to face and vanquish her dragons. The light is brighter; there is background noise and more words. A war is being waged. Some words are violent words from Frankie's father when his will is thwarted and he once again threatens Lizzie. Lizzie must acknowledge and face the fears that have kept her in bondage and allow the courage that has been

---

[24] Ibid. 267.

[25] Ibid.

silently germinating, nurtured by the love and support of those around her, to arise. Lizzie does not turn and run this time, but draws on her newly found courage and denies him.

New Vision

For both Lizzie and Orual, the vanquishing of the old brings about restoration and new beginnings. After the emptying of her pride and her rebellion abandoned, Orual is finally in a condition where she can hear the gods when they speak.[26] She acknowledges, "I could mend my soul no more than I could mend my face, unless the gods helped."[27] Orual experiences a vision in which she presents her complaint to the council of gods. As she reads the litany of the wrongs she believes she has suffered at their hands, her true self and her true voice are heard. Not only can she not deceive the gods, but she cannot deceive herself. The last vestiges of her false construction of self come crashing down and she realizes "I saw well why the gods do not speak to us openly, nor let us answer. Till that word can be dug out of us, why should they hear the babble that we think we mean? How

---

[27] Ibid, 281.

can they meet us face to face till we have faces?"[28] Her spiritual transformation and physical journey are complete, and at the end of her life, she sees the beauty in herself that was always hidden by the pride which obscured.

While both Orual's physical life and spiritual transformation are completed at the same time, Lizzie's transformation brings about a new chapter. *Dear Frankie* ends with Lizzie discovering Frankie at the bay sitting at the end of the pier. Sitting down beside him and leaning against him, the scene closes with the two sitting there, which Frankie described at the beginning of the film as "the end of the world." It is the end of that world for them, one which had been lived in fear and filled with deception, and the beginning of a new based on a foundation of truth. However, the viewer is not given a neatly wrapped ending and resolution. Lizzie's journey is ongoing; her destination not yet determined.

The Apostle Paul assures us in Romans 8:28 that in spite of circumstances, God is working together all things for our good. Good does not always mean pleasant. Good in this context means transforming us into the image of Christ. Like Orual

---

[28] Ibid, 294.

who was knocked down and trampled by the golden-wooled rams in the field of her vision (representing the acts of the gods), she found herself "butted and trampled . . . Yet they did not kill me. When they had gone over me, I lived and knew myself, and presently could stand on my feet."[29] Life can, and often does, run us over, but it is at times that very discouragement and defeat that ultimately brings us to a place of victory. Just as Lizzie and Frankie had come "to the end of the world," it is when we come to the end of ourselves that God can begin. It is the stories of individual transformation, where the weak are made strong and the corrupt are made right, that need to be told because it is only through our individual transformation . . . the making of a hero . . . that society as a whole can be redeemed.

Tales of Courage and Hope: Hamilton in Middle Earth and Narnia: Part One & Part Two

Seth Myers on the Connections from Oxford to Broadway

Hey yo, I'm just like my country
I'm young scrappy and hungry
And I'm not throwing away my shot"[1]

By means of all created things, without exception,

the divine assails us, penetrates us, and molds us.

We imagined it as distant and inaccessible,

---

[1] *Hamilton*, lyrics by Lin-Manuel Miranda (United States: Atlantic Recording, 2015). Act I, Song 3 "My Shot."

whereas in act we live steeped in its burning layers.[2]

~ Teilhard de Chardin

It is said of the developing world that "intelligence is equally distributed; opportunity is not." In their own way, the 2015 Broadway musical *Hamilton* and the 2018 film *Black Panther* address the same issue: the plight of races marginalized by history. While *Black Panther* gives its focus to Africans, both at home and abroad, *Hamilton* relives the tale of the American Founding Father, Alexander Hamilton, himself an immigrant and an orphan, arriving in New York from the Caribbean island of Nevis and rising to become the first United States Secretary of the Treasury. But *Hamilton* is cast nearly entirely with Black, Hispanic and Asian actors and actresses (save King George), and by using rap, R&B, and hip-hop, director Lin Manuel-Miranda (himself of Puerto Rican ancestry) uses *Hamilton* to open up American history to all. By identifying American Revolutionaries primarily as Blacks and Hispanics, Miranda not only makes American history theirs, but also connects the

---

[2] Pierre Teilhard de Chardin, *The Divine Milieu* (1957), quoted in Jeffrey Overstreet, *Through a Screen Darkly* (Ventura California: Regal Books, 2007), 5.

history of immigrants and marginalized races to that of America itself, "that great unfinished symphony." [3]

In this companion piece to the *Black Panther* review, we will examine the same set of themes in the play *Hamilton*: the struggle for significance by individuals, the marginalization of entire groups, and issues of race, gender, family, fatherhood, love, and the hope and courage with which these challenges are met. Once again, we will put film and stage in dialogue with theology and consider how C.S. Lewis and his Oxford colleague and fellow novelist, J.R.R. Tolkien, handled the same issues.

Hamilton: Young, Scrappy, and Hungry . . . and the World's Gonna Know His Name

Like *Black Panther*, *Hamilton* offers a story laden with courage and hope set amidst fears and missteps. *Hamilton* follows the life of Alexander Hamilton, the "Founding Father whose story never gets told," as he rises against all odds from his start as an orphaned immigrant, becomes a senior aide to General George Washington in the Revolutionary War, writes extensively promoting the Constitution, and finally becomes the first

---

[3] *Hamilton*, II.22, "The World was Wide Enough."

Secretary of the Treasury of the United States. Hamilton equates himself with colonial America, or any group seeking its place in history, as he declares,

> Hey yo, I'm just like my country
>
> I'm young, scrappy, and hungry
>
> And I'm not throwing away my shot

Hamilton brings American history, with all its hopes and revolutionary fire, alive. New York Times Reviewer Ben Brantley describes Hamilton as using rap, hip-hop, and R&B ballads to bring to life "long-dead white men" with black and Hispanic actors who "don't exactly look like the marble statues of the men they're portraying," speaking with "a fervid mix of contemporary street talk, wild and florid declarations of ambition, and oh yes, elegant phrases from momentous political documents you studied in school, like Washington's Farewell Address."[4] *Hamilton* thus comes to embody the story of today's immigrant and minority member.

---

[4] Ben Brantley, "'Hamilton,' Young Rebels Changing History and Theater," *New York Times*, August 6, 2015. https://www.nytimes.com/2015/08/07/theater/review-hamilton-young-rebels-changing-history-and-theater.html.

The musical opens with Aaron Burr, whose career is entwined with Hamilton's throughout, introducing a young Alexander Hamilton with:

How does a bastard, orphan, son of a whore
and a Scotsman,

Dropped in the middle of a forgotten

Spot in the Caribbean

by providence, impoverished, in squalor,

grow up to be a hero and a scholar?[5]

A hopeful immigrant, the young Hamilton took a collection for his travel expenses, even jump-starting his own writing career with "his first refrain, a testament to his pain."[6] Others add that he "got a lot farther, by working a lot harder, by being a self-starter, by fourteen they placed him in charge of a trading charter."[7] Hamilton's precocious mind and legendary work ethic ("this kid is insane")[8] parallel the legendary drive and work ethic of American immigrants – "immigrants – we

---

[5] *Hamilton*, I.1 "Alexander Hamilton."

[6] Ibid., I.1.

[7] Ibid.

[8] Ibid.

get the job done!"[9] He is driven by the expectation that "the world is gonna' know [his] name."[10]

To have your name known - this desire fits with the current definitions of poverty, which now include isolation from society.[11] So strong is this desire for connection that in rural areas like sub-Saharan Africa and India, where groups are involved in bringing electricity via solar energy to the 1.2 billion people who currently lack such, the overwhelming initial choice of uses for such electricity is for communication devices, such as cell phones, internet service, radio and television.[12]

But this desire in us is much stronger than simply for the world to "know your name;" to be known by God himself - this is where the Christian faith speaks most strongly to us. The Judeo-Christian tradition pioneered individual rights, as all were held equal before the Jewish law, but the Christian writer C.S. Lewis shows just how significant the individual truly is. In his famous

---

[9] Ibid., 1.20, "Yorktown."

[10] Ibid.

[11] http://www.unesco.org/new/en/social-and-human-sciences/themes/international-migration/glossary/poverty/.

[12] The author has some experience in this area, through groups such as www.ieee-smart-village.org and www.se4all.org.

Weight of Glory sermon of 1941, Lewis concluded his discussion with:

> There are no ordinary people. You have never talked to a mere mortal. Nations, cultures, arts, civilizations – these are mortal, and their life is to ours as the life of a gnat[13]

Invoking more poetic, celestial imagery, Lewis makes the point more spectacularly in *Perelandra*, from his sci-fi Space *Trilogy*, describing how,

> speech was turned into sight . . . he thought he saw the Great Dance. It seemed to be woven out of the intertwining undulation of many cords or bands of light, leaping over and under one another and mutually embraced in arabesques and flower-like subtleties . . . he could see also wherever the ribbons or serpents of light intersected, minute corpuscles of momentary brightness: and he knew somehow that these particles were the secular generalities of which history tells us – peoples, institutions, climates of opinion, civilizations, arts, sciences, and the like – ephemeral coruscations that piped their short song and vanished . . . far above these in girth

---

[13] C.S. Lewis, "Weight of Glory" in *Weight of Glory and other Addresses*, ed. Walter Hooper (New York: MacMillan, 1980), 19.

and luminosity and flashing with colors from beyond our spectrum were the lines of the personal beings, yet as different from one another in splendor as all of them from the previous class.[14]

Lewis ultimately grounds individual value in Scripture. Contrasting the Christian faith with pantheism, which requires a complete loss of identity in a final union with the otherwise impersonal cosmos, Lewis reminds us of Revelation 2:17 in which each saint is given a new name in heaven:

> What can be more a man's own than this new name which even in eternity remains a secret between God and him? And what shall we take this secrecy to mean? Surely, that each of the redeemed shall forever know and praise some aspect of the divine beauty better than any other creature can. Why else were individuals created but that God, loving all infinitely, should love each differently . . . If all experienced God in the same way and returned Him an identical worship . .

---

[14] C.S. Lewis, *Perelandra* (New York: Scribner, 2003), 187.

. it would be like an orchestra in which all the instruments played the same note.[15]

But just as the American Republic is guided by the motto *e pluribus unum* (out of the many, one), the republic of Heaven reverses the score: from the One, many. It is not only in Divine family relations of the Trinity that a community is found whose hallmark is love, but as we are adopted into this family ("heirs of God, joint-heirs with Christ," Romans 8:17), we experience the joy of being with the many. Lewis's orchestra of the saints has its earthly foretaste, in at least a secular sense, in Hamilton's description of "America, you great unfinished symphony . . . a place where even orphan immigrants can leave their fingerprints and rise up."[16]

And the One doesn't just give way to the camaraderie of the many, as in *Hamilton*'s symphony or even Lewis' orchestra; the Divine Orchestra Director pursues each member like the proverbial *Hound of Heaven*.[17] Just as Lewis's Aslan, a Christ figure in Narnia who follows "I give you

---

[15] C.S. Lewis, *The Problem of Pain*, (New York: Collier, 1986), 149-150. Ch. 10 "Heaven."

[16] *Hamilton*, II.22 "The World Was Wide Enough."

[17] Francis Thompson, "The Hound of Heaven" in *Oxford Book of English Mystical Verse*, 1917.

yourselves" with "I give you myself,"[18] or Lewis's waterfall in *The Great Divorce* which "stood, like one crucified, against the rocks and poured himself perpetually down towards the forest with great joy,"[19] so does the one, true God pursue us to the point of sending Christ (Himself) as the heart of this orchestra, to dwell in the heart of each player. Lewis also captures this sense of God as the sovereign who pursues us in the following passage:

> Men are reluctant to pass over from the notion of an abstract and negative deity to the living God. I do not wonder. Here lies the deepest tap-root of Pantheism and of the objection to traditional imagery . . . The Pantheist's God does nothing, demands nothing. He is there if you wish for Him, like a book on a shelf. He will not pursue you. There is no danger that at any time heaven and earth should flee away at His glance. If He were the truth, then we could really say that all the Christian images-of kingship were a historical accident of which our religion ought to be cleansed . . . It is always shocking to meet life where we thought we were alone. "Lookout!" we cry, "it's

---

[18] C.S. Lewis, *The Magician's Nephew* (Norwalk, CT: Easton Press, 1983), 128. Ch. 10.

[19] C.S. Lewis, *The Great Divorce* (New York: HarperOne, 2000), 49.

alive." . . . An "impersonal God" - well and good. A subjective God of beauty, truth and goodness, inside our own heads – better still. A formless life-force surging through us, a vast power which we can tap – best of all. **But God Himself, alive, pulling at the other end of the cord, perhaps approaching at an infinite speed, the hunter, king, husband - that is quite another matter.**[20]

Hamilton's quest "to have his name known," to "not throw away his shot" on the stage of history, is merely a whisper compared to the song on the stage for the Divine Audience with whom we can find our significance. This is not to disparage the need for significance by groups ignored and mistreated throughout history, but is intended to place that yearning in its full context, the "burning layers" of the "divine (which) assails us"[21] of which Teilhard de Chardin informs us. *Hamilton* represents a sociological extrapolation of Augustine's famous dictum, "You have made us for yourself, and our heart is restless until it rests in you."[22]

---

[20] C.S. Lewis, *Miracles* (New York: Collier, 1978), 93-94.

[21] See footnote 2.

[22] Augustine, *Confessions*, I.1.

Quest and Questions of Significance

The young Hamilton overcomes further hardships, such as his father leaving at age ten and his mother dying two years later, requiring him to move in with a cousin who soon commits suicide. His landowner asks him to manage his farm and trading activities, which gives the young islander his first opportunity. Hamilton had long dreamt of such an opportunity: "As a kid in the Caribbean I wished for a war. I knew that I was poor. I knew it was the only way to . . . rise up!"[23]

"Rise up!" - this anthem repeats throughout *Hamilton*. But it is more than a call to political revolution; it is a call to what lies *behind* every revolution - the chance to be heard, to be significant, and to be part of "the great conversation," as opposed to a bystander, if not a floormat. The young Hamilton rises above his early setbacks, which "left him with nothin' but ruined pride, something new inside, a voice inside saying 'you gotta fend for yourself,'"[24] (and after which "he started retreatin, and readin' every treatise on the shelf"). And behind this "ruined pride" lay

---

[23] *Hamilton*, I.8 "Right Hand Man."

[24] *Hamilton*, I.1.

something deeper, even more fundamental: a desire to belong, to have someone, if only history long after he is gone, know his name. The young Hamilton "inside was longing for something to be a part of, the brother was ready to beg, steal, borrow or barter."[25]

Lewis and Tolkien both speak of this need for significance. Tolkien showed how the question of significance lies deep within us in his poem *Mythopoeia*, penned in 1931 after an evening discussion with Lewis on the truth and power of the Christian story:

Yes! `wish-fulfilment dreams' we spin to cheat

our timid hearts and ugly Fact defeat!

Whence came the wish, and whence the power
to dream,

or some things fair and others ugly deem?

All wishes are not idle, not in vain

fulfilment we devised.[26]

---

[25] *Hamilton*, I.1.

[26] J.R.R. Tolkien, *Mythopoeia*, 1931. The poem was written to Lewis after an evening's walk and discussion about how the Christian story had the power of myth, but was a myth that actually happened. The place was Addison's Walk, a path on the grounds of

Tolkien thus turns the tables on figures like Freud who see God as mere wish-fulfilment. Rather than simply wishing God into existence, it is our need to wish – for beauty, for God – that demands an answer. Tolkien follows the modern philosophy professor who, in response to the student's question as to whether or not he even existed, gave the response, "And who, shall I say, is asking? Neither rocks nor streams nor dogs ask, 'Why?'"

Lewis, as well, would later argue as much himself. Taking a cue, it would seem, from Tolkien (see above: "Whence came the wish, and whence the power to dream, some things fair and others ugly deem"), Lewis argues that our sense of beauty, and in fact our very moral sense, comes from what some have termed our "sensus divinitatas" grounded in our "imago dei" – our divine sense, stemming from our having been made in the image of God. It was precisely the judgment that certain things were good, and especially that others were evil, that confounded the young, non-Christian Lewis, ultimately spurring him on in his journey to faith. In the essay *De Futilitate*, while arguing that the mind could not make sense of the scientific

---

Oxford's Magdalen College; the poem can be found online at
http://home.agh.edu.pl/~evermind/jrrtolkien/mythopoeia.htm.

world were it not imbued with the same intelligence built into the laws of math and science, Lewis finds our sense of morality, meaning, and justice to be just as crucial:

> There is, to be sure, one glaringly obvious ground for denying that any moral purpose at all is operative in the universe . . . the actual course of events in all its wasteful cruelty and apparent indifference, or hostility, to life. But then . . . . that is precisely the ground which we cannot use.

> Unless we judge this waste and cruelty to be real evils we cannot of course condemn the universe for exhibiting them. Unless we take our own standard of goodness to be valid in principle . . . we cannot mean anything by calling waste and cruelty evils . . . unless we allow ultimate reality to be moral, we cannot morally condemn it.

> The more seriously we take our own charge of futility the more we are committed to the implication that reality in the last resort is not futile at all. *The defiance of the good atheist hurled at an apparently ruthless and idiotic cosmos is really an unconscious homage to something in or behind that cosmos which he*

> *recognizes at infinitely valuable and authoritative*[27]

One's story should matter to history; it should matter in this life as well. The poetic heights to which this conviction rises (up!) drives *Hamilton*. Hamilton's passion against injustice finds a resonance in Lewis, as he continues, "I cannot and never could persuade myself that such defiance is displeasing to the supreme mind. There is something holier about the atheism of a Shelley than about the theism of a Paley. That is the lesson of the book of Job."[28]

Revolutionaries are thus, as Lewis argues, theologically in vogue.

Courage and its Source

Hamilton's courage draws not just from wanting his voice to be heard, but also from his sense of justice, of right(s) and wrong. Hamilton and Burr are repeatedly offered as stark contrasts in courage and cowardice, Burr wondering of Hamilton, "Why do you always say what you believe?" and Hamilton asking, "If you stand for

---

[27] C.S. Lewis, "De Futilitate" in *Christia Reflections* (Grand Rapids, MI: Eerdmans, 1975), 69-70.

[28] Ibid.

nothing, Burr, what'll you fall for?"[29] When the young Alexander Hamilton and friends throw in their fates with the cause of the Revolutionary War, courageously declaring, "I may not live to see our glory, but I will gladly join the fight,"[30] Burr backs away. He is "willing to wait for it:" to wait for the British officer's wife, with whom he is having an affair, to become his, and to wait for after the war "when everyone who loves me has died" to find the reason for his own survival.[31] And while Burr stakes his pragmatism on how "I am the one thing in life I can control," and declares, "I'm not standing still, I'm lying in wait," he sees that "Hamilton doesn't hesitate. He exhibits no restraint. He takes and he takes and he takes and he keeps winning anyway."[32] Hamilton's feisty courage shows itself further when, despite his "skill with the quill being undeniable," he "wants to fight, not write"[33] and take a position of command, which Washington refuses.

---

[29] *Hamilton*, I.2 "Aaron Burr, Sir."

[30] *Hamilton*, I.4 "The Story of Tonight."

[31] *Hamilton*, I.13 "Wait for It."

[32] Ibid.

[33] *Hamilton*, I.9, "A Winter's Ball."

Courage in the face of chaos: the Director Miranda invokes the classic imagery of Shakespeare's *Macbeth* to underscore Hamilton's classic plight of the struggle for right.

Tomorrow and tomorrow and tomorrow

Creeps in this petty place from day to day"

I trust you'll understand my reference to

Another Scottish tragedy without my having

to name the play

They think me Macbeth, and ambition is my folly

I'm a polymath, a pain in the ass, a massive pain

Madison is Banquo, Jefferson's Macduff,

And Birnam Wood is Congress on its way to Dunsinane.[34]

Hamilton has quoted *MacBeth* at the point in the play where MacBeth's confidence is shaken due to hearing of Lady Macbeth's death and what appears to be the movement of Birnam Wood toward Dunsinane Castle where Macbeth is

---

[34] *Hamilton*, II.3, "Take a Break."

waiting. This speech is perhaps the most famous from *Macbeth*, echoing in its final lines the same sort of amoral chaos against which Hamilton finds himself, inspiring a courageous quest for justice and sanity.

Tomorrow and tomorrow and tomorrow

Creeps in this petty pace from day to day

To the last syllable of recorded time,

And all our yesterdays have lighted fools

The way to dusty death. Out, out, brief candle!

Life's but a walking shadow, a poor player

That struts and frets his hour upon the stage

And then is heard no more. It is a tale

Told by an idiot, full of sound and fury,

Signifying nothing.[35]

Hamilton pushes on in the face of such chaos and destruction and flourishes because of his courage. Lewis explains:

Courage is not simply one of the virtues, but the form of every virtue at the testing point, which means at the point of its

---

[35] Shakespeare, *Macbeth* Act V, Scene 5, 22-31.

highest reality. A chastity or honesty, or mercy, which yields to danger will be chaste or honest or merciful only on conditions.[36]

Tolkien poetically describes such courage, as well, in his poem *Mythopoeia* written to Lewis, a poem which brings up images from his *Lord of the Rings* saga at various points:

Blessed are the timid hearts that evil hate,

that quail in its shadow, and yet shut the gate;

that seek no parley, and in guarded room,

through small and bare, upon a clumsy loom

weave rissues gilded by the far-off day

hoped and believed in under Shadow's sway.

Blessed are the men of Noah's race that build

their little arks, though frail and poorly filled,

and steer through winds contrary towards a wraith,

a rumour of a harbour guessed by faith.[37]

---

[36] C.S. Lewis, *Screwtape Letters* (New York: Harper Collins, 2000), Ch. 29, 161.

[37] Tolkien, *Mythopoeia*, 1931.

Courage, arguably the chief virtue of Tolkien's *Lord of the Rings*, is found in both daring battles against massive odds and in the dogged, persistent will to reach Mount Doom with the Ring. Tolkien found inspiration for this in Norse mythology, where gods and men were pitted together against destruction from monsters. Unlike the gods from Greek and Roman myths, who are, "not besieged, not in ever-present peril or under future doom,"[38] the Norse gods of Iceland, Denmark et.al. were "within time, doomed with their allies to death. Their battle is with the monsters and the outer darkness. They gather heroes for the last defense."[39] While the Southern gods are thus

> more godlike – more lofty, more dread . . .
> timeless and do not fear death . . . It is the
> strength of the northern mythological
> imagination that it faced this problem
> (death, annihilation),[40] put the monsters

---

[38] J.R.R. Tolkien, "The Monsters and the Critics" in *The Monsters and the Critics and Other Essays* (London: Harper Collins, 2006), 25.

[39] Ibid.

[40] Parenthesis is mine; the theme of death and annihilation follow Tolkien's comments about the significance of his Lord of the Rings epic, "It is about death, mainly" written in a letter of 14th October, 1958; it also follows his theme of *eucatastrophe* as "joyous deliverance" from "sorrow and failure," in short, "the Great Escape: the Escape from Death." (Tolkien, "On Fairy Stories" in *The Monsters and the Critics and Other Essays*, 153.)

in the center, gave them victory but no honor, and *found a potent but terrible solution in naked will and courage.* "As a working theory absolutely impregnable."[41]

Tolkien finds yet another strength of Norse mythology, the poem *Beowulf* in particular, which he single-handedly revived for critical appraisal, in Christian Scripture. Passages in *Beowulf* relating giants in a war with God, along with two mentions of "the undoubtedly Scriptural Cain" as the ancestor of the giants and Grendel particularly, Tolkien claims have special significance:

> At this point new Scripture and old tradition touched and ignited . . . Man alien in a hostile world, engaged in a struggle which he cannot win while the world lasts, is assured that his foes are the foes also of Dryhten, **that his courage noble in itself is also the highest loyalty**[42]

The courage of Hamilton thus parallels that of Beowulf in this sense: they have the same faith and

---

[41] Ibid, 25-26.

[42] Ibid., 26.

hope in a justice and goodness that they find lacking in their world.

Hamilton & Burr : Courage and its Counterpart

The courageous and bold Hamilton has a perfectly cowardly, calculating counterpart in Burr. Together, they demonstrate Lewis' own statements on courage and cowardice:

> Cowardice, alone of all the vices, is purely painful – horrible to anticipate, horrible to feel, horrible to remember ... to make a wound deep in his charity, you should therefore first defeat his courage.[43]

> Courage is not simply one of the virtues, but the form of every virtue at the testing point, which means at the point of its highest reality. A chastity or honesty, or mercy, which yields to danger will be chaste or honest or merciful only on conditions. Pilate was merciful till it became risky.[44]

In their initial meeting, the elder Burr advises young Alexander to "talk less, smile more / Don't let

---

[43] Lewis, *Screwtape Letters*, 160.

[44] Ibid., 161.

them know what you're against and what you're for."[45]

When Hamilton makes his name after the war in taking stands at Constitutional Convention as a delegate from New York, Burr half admires him – "Why do you write like you're running out of time?" – and half condemns him - "Why do you always say what you believe?"[46] Hamilton's later retort is just as telling: "If you stand for nothing, Burr, what'll you fall for?"[47]

Counter to the cowardice of Pilate that Lewis describes, Burr says of Hamilton, "Hamilton doesn't hesitate. He exhibits no restraint. He takes and he takes and he takes and he keeps winning anyway. He changes the game. He plays and he raises the stakes."[48] By contrast, Burr simply "wait(s) for it,"[49] hoping to find opportunity at the least costly price.

Hamilton's derring-do shows in the war effort, where he becomes Washington's right hand man, aiding the Revolution, which is "outgunned,

---

[45] *Hamilton*, "Aaron Burr, Sir," I.2.

[46] *Hamilton*, "Non-Stop," I.23.

[47] *Hamilton*, "Room Where It Happens," II.5.

[48] *Hamilton*, "Wait for It," 1.13.

[49] Ibid.

outmanned,   outnumbered,   out   planned,"[50]
underfinanced and faltering. Hamilton accepts the
role, but squabbles with Washington, as he wants
to head up a regiment: "Hamilton still wants to
fight, not write, [though] Hamilton's skill with a
quill is undeniable." Hamilton writes to Congress
for more supplies, writes polemics against slavery,
and even steals cannons from the British. Burr does
not join in and says farewell to Hamilton until after
the war, partly due to his living with the wife of a
British officer.

After the war, Hamilton resumes his law
practice, rising quickly so that he becomes one of
New   York's   delegates   to   the   Constitutional
Convention "Maaaaan, the man is non-stop!"[51]
Every day, he "writes like he's running out of time."
Hamilton's biggest battle, however, becomes the
charge   Washington   gives   him   after   being
appointed Secretary of Treasury: to get his proposal
for the Federal Government to assume states' debts
through Congress, thus extending credit to the
states to fund their own economies. Hamilton runs
into opposition from the South and the powerful
Virginia   delegation   in   particular   –   Thomas

---

[50] *Hamilton*, "Right Hand Man," I.8.

[51] *Hamilton*, "Non Stop," I.23.

Jefferson and James Madison. Agrarian Southern states are wealthier than their Northern brothers, though likely due to slave labor, as Hamilton reminds them, "Hey neighbor, your debt's paid cuz you don't pay for labor . . . yeah keep ranting, we know who's doing the planting."[52] In a closed meeting, Hamilton somehow brokers a deal, against all odds, so that "the immigrant emerges with unprecedented financial power, a system he can shape however he wants" while the Virginians walk away with the Capitol getting moved from New York City to Virginia (the present day Washington D.C.).

Hamilton's courage distinguishes itself from Burr's cowardice throughout the story. Alexander's legendary is demonstrated by writing a series of pamphlets, The Federalist Papers, defending the new United States Constitution, along with John Jay and James Madison. Burr refuses to help, Jay gets sick after writing five, Madison writes twenty-nine, and Hamilton writes an astounding fifty-one. By contrast, Burr's resume reeks of calculated opportunism. He switches political parties for personal gain (defeating Hamilton's father-in-law Philip Schuyler for the Senate seat from New York),

---

[52] *Hamilton*, "Cabinet Battle #1," II.2.

and cannot fully commit to the side of the American Revolution, due in no small part to his courting a British officer's wife. Burr's name ultimately has been associated with the treason for which he was indicted but acquitted, seeking the personal gain of possibly a separate nation carved out of the American West. Hamilton ultimately denounces Burr, as we will see later; as Lewis noted, watching cowardice is painful, particularly for the courageous.

Belonging: Race, Gender and Family

This deep need for significance, for belonging, further drives such storylines as racial fairness, gender, family and love. Of race, the young Alexander writes about the abolition of slavery, though the most poignant lines are given to fellow revolutionary Lauren's:

> *But we'll never be truly free*
>
> *until those in bondage have the same rights as you and me,*
>
> *You and I. Do or die. Wait till I*
>
> *sally in on a stallion*
>
> *with the first black battalion.*

It should be noted, however, that modern historians take some issue with the historical Hamilton and that of the play. Miranda based the play on the 2004 book by freelance journalist Ron Chernow, *Alexander Hamilton,*[53] but criticisms have been made that the actual Hamilton was not quite the abolitionist portrayed in the play.[54]

In regards to race, Lewis held a special place for all ethnicities. In his *Space Trilogy*, a persistent theme is the redemption of the better part of humanity from its distortion, of the poetic, Logres of the Arthurian legends of Britain from the petty shopkeepers of modern England. Thus, he states:

> Of course, there are universal rules to which all goodness must conform. But that's only the grammar of virtue. It's not there that the sap is. He doesn't make two blades of grass the same: how much less two saints, two nations, two angels. The whole work of healing Tellus (earth) depends on nursing that little spark, on incarnating that ghost, which is still alive in every real people, and different in each.

---

[53] Ron Chernow, *Hamilton* (New York: Penguin, 2004).

[54] Reed, Ishmael (August 21, 2015). "'Hamilton: the Musical': Black Actors Dress Up like Slave Traders...and It's Not Halloween". *CounterPunch*. Archived from the original on August 26, 2015. Retrieved November 28, 2016

> When Logres really dominates Britain,
> when the goddess Reason, the divine
> clearness, is really enthroned in France,
> when the order of Heaven is really
> followed in China – why, then it will be
> spring.[55]

Of gender, in *Hamilton* the Schuyler sisters both voice and demonstrate the strengths of their sex, calling for their own share of recognition and equality from history. Alexander first meets the eldest of the Schuyler sisters, Angelica, though he marries the younger Eliza.[56] Angelica admits to reading *Common Sense* by Thomas Paine, and declares that when she meets Thomas Jefferson, to his "All men are created equal," she declares "I'm a compel him to include women in the sequel!"[57] After the sisters declare they are out to find in their men "a mind at work," Angelica recounts later of her meeting Hamilton that, "So this is what it's like to match wits / with someone at your level . . . it's / the feeling of freedom, of seein' the light / it's Ben Franklin with a key and a kite!"[58]

---

[55] C.S. Lewis, *That Hideous Strength* (New York: Scribner, 2003), 369.

[56] In fact there were fifteen Schuyler children; a third sister Peggy makes it into *Hamilton*, but has a minor role.

[57] *Hamilton*, I.5, "The Schuyler Sisters."

[58] *Hamilton*, I.11, "Satisfied."

As gender gives way to the larger consideration of family, Angelica and Eliza exhibit every bit the strength and fight as their male revolutionary counterparts, but for home and family rather than "God and country." Angelica sacrificially passes Alexander along to her younger sister Eliza upon realizing how smitten ("helpless!") she was with him, though she had herself fallen in love with him and knows Eliza would have quietly and sacrificially done the same for her.[59] And as Alexander's career demands increasing portions of his attention, Eliza fights just as heroically for their family life in beckoning him to pay attention to young Philip their son, and "take a break / run away with us for the summer. Let's go upstate, there's a lake I know . . ."[60]

Even the male leads, Hamilton and Burr, yearn for the belonging found in family as well. Alexander finds in love and family a meaning entirely outside of revolution and politics, confiding in Eliza that:

---

[59] Once again, Miranda took some historical liberties for the sake of drama, as Angelica was in fact already married for two years and by then had two of her eventual eight children.

[60] *Hamilton*, II.3 "Take a Break."

"Insane, your family brings out a different side of me

No stress, my love for you is never in doubt, / we'll get a little place in Harlem and we'll figure it out

I've been living without a family since I was a child, / my father left, my mother died, I grew up buck wild

But I'll never forget my mother's face, that was real "

Eliza affirms the place of home and family when she informs Alexander she is pregnant with their first child, after writing Washington to send him home:

So long as you come home at the end of the day

That would be enough.

We don't need a legacy,

We don't need money …

If you could let me inside your heart,

Oh, let me be a part of the narrative

In the story they will write someday.

Let this moment be the first chapter:

Where you decide to stay

And I could be enough

And we could be enough

That would be enough.[61]

And just as T'Challa and Stevens aka Killmonger in *Black Panther* dealt with the mistakes of their fathers, Burr and Hamilton find in their own children the opportunity to provide what their missing fathers could not provide them. Alexander finds "so much more inside" him than just "pride" when with his son Philip, who "outshines the morning sun" and "when he smiles I fall apart." Likewise, Burr's daughter Theodosia's smile "knocks (him) out . . . makes (him) fall apart (though) I thought I was so smart." Ultimately both Burr and Hamilton are driven by this love to "make the world safe and sound for you . . . we'll bleed and fight for you, we'll make it right for you."[62] The courage of both Hamilton and Burr in paving a world for their families is born not just from a

---

[61] *Hamilton*, I.17, "That Would be Enough,."

[62] *Hamilton*, "Dear Theodosia," I.22.

strong desire for justice and righting wrongs, but in providing for their loved ones.

A singular, pithy comment from Lewis affirms his view of the primacy of family. In a letter to a Mrs. Johnson in 1955, Lewis stated, "A housewife's work . . . is surely, in reality, the most important work in the world . . . your job is the one for which all others exist."[63] Expanding on the thought, Lewis also there queried:

> "What do ships, railways, mines, cars, government etc. exist for except that people may be fed, warmed, and safe in their own homes? As Dr. Johnson said, "To be happy at home is the end of all human endeavor" . . . We wage war in order to have peace, we work in order to have leisure, we produce food in order to eat it."[64]

In his own way, Tolkien affirmed as much, drawing a simple, contented picture of life in the Shire:

> The Shire at this time had hardly any government. Families for the most part

---

[63] March 16, 1955 letter to Mrs. John son, full context at http://www.essentialcslewis.com/2016/01/23/ccslq-19-homemakerultimate-career/.

[64] Ibid.

managed their own affairs. Growing food and eating it occupied most of their time. In other matters they were, as a rule, generous and not greedy, but contented and moderate, so that estates, farms, workshops and small trades tended to remain unchanged for generations.[65]

We thus see how the pathos of Hamilton - pathos in the courage to forge a free nation, pathos in fighting for a sense of belonging against the tides of history, pathos in seeking a place for races, gender and family - is compelling and moving. But these are issues that have been contemplated and spoken on by serious thinkers for generations, and we have seen how Lewis and Tolkien provide their own wisdom on these matters. We thus conclude part one of our look at Hamilton in conversation with Tolkien and Lewis. In part two, we will continue our comparison of *Hamilton* with Tolkien's Middle Earth and Lewis' Narnia and other writings by examining love and gender in more detail, as well as solace and finally, our place in history and where we best find meaning and significance.

---

[65] J.R.R. Tolkien, *The Hobbit* (New York: Ballantine, 1986), 30.

- PART II -

We continue our look at Hamilton from the perspective of Oxford Professors C.S. Lewis and J.R.R. Tolkien. Part one showed how issues of group and individual significance, courage and cowardice, and race, gender, and family are prominent in Hamilton, and that Lewis and Tolkien both had some significant things to say about these issues. We now turn to love, a key factor in issues of gender and family in particular, and look more in depth at what Lewis had to say about explicitly about it.

Belonging: Love

Finally, and briefly, of love: where it is implicit in *Hamilton*, Lewis gives the full definition. Love is at the heart of marriage and family, as we can see when Eliza beckons Alexander that, "So long as you come home at the end of the day, that would be enough."[66] But Alexander and Eliza's sister Angelica both confess to personal ambitions which will never be satisfied.[67] Quite arguably, this stems from an inadequate conception of love, a love that

---

[66] *Hamilton*, I.17, "That Would Be Enough."

[67] *Hamilton*, I.11, "Satisfied."

is grounded in self rather than in something larger. In his spiritual autobiography *Surprised by Joy*, Lewis confessed that his unrepentant ambition was to satisfy his own soul, alone: "Remember, I had always wanted (mad wish!) to call my soul my own."[68] But when this is the only possible foundation for love, eventually one wishes to call other's souls one's own as well. Thus, Lewis describes "smother love" in his *Great Divorce*, particularly in chapter ten in where the love of the controlling mother becomes:

> What she calls her love for her son has turned into a poor, prickly, astringent sort of the thing. But there's still a wee spark of something that's not just herself in it. That might be blown into a flame.[69]

At one point in *The Great Divorce*, Lewis even brings a stampede of unicorns onto the scene with the hope that, for just one moment, a self-love absorbed individual might take their mind off of themself. Lewis goes on to state the case for the true ground of love more explicitly with, "Human beings can't make one another really happy for long

---

[68] C.S.Lewis, *Surprised by Joy* (Glasgow: Collins, 1955), 182.

[69] C.S. Lewis, *The Great Divorce* (New York: Harper Collins, 2001), 104.

. . . You cannot fully love another creature fully until you love God."[70]

Lewis makes the same point when he distinguishes between "Need-love" and "Gift-love" in his *Four Loves*: Need-love is all about oneself, while Gift-love is concerned solely with the good of its recipient. Lewis models Gift-love by describing its divine source:

> The Father gives all He is and has to the Son. The Son gives Himself back to the Father, and gives Himself to the world.[71]

And this is arguably the singular insight of what he considered his greatest fictional work, *Till We Have Faces*. The jealous, plain-faced sister Orual comes to realize that she had had only "smother love" for her younger, beautiful sister Psyche:

> Oh Psyche, oh goddess . . . Never again will I call you mine; but all there is of me shall be yours. Alas, you now know what it's worth. I never wished you well, never had one selfless thought of you. I was a craver.[72]

---

[70] Ibid., 99-100.

[71] C.S. Lewis, *The Four Loves* (New York: Harcourt, 1991), 1.

[72] C.S. Lewis, *Till We Have Faces* (New York: Harcourt, 1985), 305.

Hamilton's richness lies in its being more than simply a story of a nation of immigrants finding belonging, as love and family are brought strongly into the narrative. While *Black Panther* focused on the role of fathers, showed strong capable women contributing to Wakandan society and allowed space for Okoye's military career within her love relation with King T'Challa, in *Hamilton* it is the pathos of love and family that gives the political narrative flesh and blood. But Lewis shows us the deeper meanings of these, explaining why *Hamilton* is more gripping, and of more enduring significance, than a simple political narrative.

In part two of this article, we continue by first examining Lewis's more developed views on love in his Space Trilogy, then look at solace in Hamilton, as it naturally follows the twin story lines of courageous battles fought and of love, and conclude with a look at how "History has its eyes on you."[73]

Lewis on Gender and Love

Lewis's views on love can hardly be considered complete without a look at his sci-fi series, *The Space Trilogy*, which might otherwise be considered a trilogy of the sexes. The opening book, *Out of the*

---

[73] *Hamilton*, I.19, "History Has its Eyes on You."

Silent Planet, is set on Malacandra (the male Mars), the sequel on Perelandra (the female Venus), while the finale is set on Thulcandra (Earth), where marriage is examined. It has been observed that the opposing community structures in *That Hideous Strength* reflect the differences between harmonious family life and a less organic world of competition.[74] Two societies oppose each other – one secular, scientific and democratic, Belbury (which houses the National Institute of Coordinated Experiments, or N.I.C.E.), and the other familial, with hierarchical but complementary roles, the Society of St. Anne's. But it is the democratic, scientific society Belbury where everyone struggles to gain the upper hand and can trust no one, whereas the patriarchal society functions more like a loving family in which everyone truly gets along! Viva la difference.

Lewis comments insightfully on gender throughout the *Space Trilogy*. Explaining the ruling spirits of Malacandra (Mars) and Perelandra (Venus), Lewis states

> The two creatures were sexless. But he of Malacandra was masculine (not male);

---

[74] Louis Markos, "Life and Writings of C.S. Lewis," *The Great Courses.* (Chantilly, VA: The Teaching Company, 2000)

she of Perelandra was feminine (not female). Malacandra seemed to him to have the look of one standing armed, at the ramparts of his own remote archaic world, in ceaseless vigilance, his eyes ever roaming the earth-ward horizon whence his danger came long ago. But the eyes of Perelandra opened, as it were, inward, as if they were the curtained gateway to a world of waves and murmurings and wandering airs, of life that rocked in winds and splashed on mossy stones and descended as the dew and arose sunward in thin-spun delicacy of mist. On Mars the very forests are of stone; in Venus the lands swim. For now he thought of them no more as Malacandra and Perelandra. He called them by their Tellurian names. With deep wonder he thought to himself, "My eyes have seen Mars and Venus. I have seen Ares and Aphrodite.[75]

The genders go beyond the sexes, however, Lewis instructs us. Noting that languages have masculine and feminine cases for all sorts of things, from mountains (male) to trees (female), Lewis argues that gender underlies language and reality: "the male and female of organic creatures are rather faint and blurred reflections of masculine

---

[75] Lewis, *Perelandra*, 171.

and feminine."[76] But they do not reduce to simple, homogenous equality. "Equality is not the deepest thing," the Director of St. Anne's tells Jane Sturbridge in the finale, *That Hideous Strength*.[77] To Jane's notion that in the soul that people were equal, the Director retorts:

> That is the last place where they are equal. Equality before the law, equality of incomes – that is very well. Equality guards life; it doesn't make it. It is medicine, not food . . . Courtship knows nothing of it; nor does fruition . . . No one has ever told you that   obedience   – humility – is an erotic necessity. You are putting equality just where it ought not be . . . You see that obedience and rule are more like a dance than a drill – specially between man and woman where the roles are always changing. [78]

So essential is this fundamental difference between the genders that Lewis has the Director state, "You do not fail in obedience through lack of love, but have lost love because you never attempted obedience."[79]

---

[76] Ibid.

[77] Lewis, *That Hideous Strength*, 145

[78] Ibid., 145 – 147.

[79] Ibid., 145.

And a greater symbolism awaits the student of gender and of Lewis. When Jane dreamed of a world of dry, homogenous equality, the Director leads her to see:

> That there might be differences all the way up, richer, sharper, even fiercer, at every rung of the ascent . . . "Yes," said the Director, "there is no escape . . . The male you could have escaped, for it exists only on the biological level. But the masculine none of us can escape. What is above and beyond all things is so masculine that we are all feminine in relation to it. You had better agree with you adversary quickly."[80]

So, when Jane asks, "You mean I shall have to become a Christian?" the Director responds, "It looks like it."[81] This supreme male gender is the supreme being which Lewis had so feared in his conversion: "I had wanted (mad wish!) 'to call my soul my own.'"[82] Concluding the paragraph in which Lewis admits he was "the most dejected and reluctant convert in all England," he considers the divine compulsion:

---

[80] Ibid., 313.

[81] Ibid.

[82] Lewis, *Surprised by Joy*, 182.

The words **compele intrare** – compel them to come in, have been so abused by wicked men that we shudder at them; but, properly understood, they plumb the depth of the Divine mercy. The hardness of God is kinder than the softness of men, and His compulsion is our liberation.[83]

Likewise, Jane (and Mark) find themselves at the mercy of "the origin of all right demands," and a God with "strong skillful hands thrust down to make, and mend, perhaps to destroy," who "is above and beyond all things . . . so masculine that we are all feminine in relation to it."[84]

Solace

Despite his personal flourishing, Hamilton creates and endures many sorrows. His affair with Maria Reynolds, occurring when he could have otherwise spent the summer with his family upstate, puts his marriage in shambles. Holding for love and family over Alexander's ambition, Eliza declares:

> *I'm erasing myself from the narrative,*
> *Let future historians wonder*
> *How Eliza reacted when you broke her heart.*

---

[83] Ibid, 183.

[84] Ibid., 313 – 315.

The world has no right to my heart.
The world has no place in our bed.
They don't get to know what I said[85]

The second devastating blow comes when their son Philip dies in a duel defending his father's name from insult. As Eliza's sister Angelica describes in the song "It's Quiet Uptown," a serene lament, "There are moments that the words don't reach, there is suffering too terrible to name."[86] Subsequently, "The Hamiltons move uptown, and learn to live with the unimaginable,"[87] and amid the ensuing quiet, Alexander finds solace in faith:

I take the children to the church on Sunday,
A sign of the cross at the door
And I pray
I never used to do that before.[88]

Angelica alludes to the same source of comfort, "There are moments that the words don't reach, There is a grace too powerful to name." Their journey through "the unimaginable" ends with the

---

[85] *Hamilton*, II.15, "Burn."

[86] *Hamilton*, II.18, "It's Quiet Uptown."

[87] Ibid.

[88] Ibid.

Hamilton in Middle Earth & Narnia

refrain, "Forgiveness. Can you imagine? Forgiveness. Can you imagine?"[89]

But where *Hamilton* stops short of explicit faith – a "grace too powerful to name" and "forgiveness, can you imagine?" – Lewis shows a Christian faith that explicitly provides the answer. Forgiveness is key to the Christian story – no other religion in the world can boast the centrality of forgiveness that the Christian faith does. It is the story of the cross, an atonement before God offering forgiveness to each member of humanity. It is central to such works as the Christian author Victor Hugo's *Les Miserables* (1862) and the 2018 film about the worship song, *I Can Only Imagine*.

It was Lewis's own Christian faith that helped him through his own portion of soul-numbing grief, the loss of his wife Joy, which he addressed in *A Grief Observed*:

> "Where is God?" Lewis asked, "Go to Him when your need is desperate, when all other hope is in vain, and what do you find? A door slammed in your face, and a sound of bolting and double-bolting from the inside. And after that, silence."[90]

---

[89] Ibid.

[90] C.S.Lewis, *A Grief Observed* (New York: Bantam, 1976), 4.

Twenty years prior to his *Grief Observed*, Lewis was asked to write a book on pain, though he admitted that he felt hardly qualified for the task. Nevertheless, he signaled the journey from pain to God that he would follow decades later in his own pain, in his *Problem of Pain*:

> Pain insists on being attended to. God whispers to us in our pleasures, speaks to us in our conscience, but shouts in our pains: it is his megaphone to rouse a deaf world . . . No doubt Pain as God's megaphone is a terrible instrument; it may lead to final and unrepented rebellion. But it gives the only opportunity the bad man can have for amendment. It removes the veil. It plants the flag of truth within the fortress of a rebel soul[91]

When in his own grief, Lewis struggled on whether to regard God as a Cosmic Sadist or Cosmic Vivisector, or even whether one should believe in a God at all. He likened the experience of pain to a card game which is only interesting if there is money on the game. Only when the stakes are high will you find out what your hand is worth, and only suffering can test your hand, by fire as it were.

---

[91] Lewis, *The Problem of Pain.* 93, 95. Ch.6 "Human Pain."

Lewis found his own expectation of God to be shallow, and came to realize that "the more we believe that God hurts only to heal, the less we can believe that there is any use in begging for tenderness."[92] Lewis came to find solace in his faith, in the hands of that great vivisector Himself. He pondered how his wife's passage from life led her to a greater glory, to be like a sharp, brilliant sword now wielded in the hand of her maker. And not only a sword,

> But also like a garden. Like a nest of gardens, wall in wall, hedge within hedge, more secret, more full of fragrant and fertile life, the further you entered in . . . In some way, in its unique way, like Him who made it.[93]

In pondering her completion, Lewis found his own salve:

> Thus up from the garden to the Gardener, from the sword to the Smith. To the life-giving Life and the Beauty that makes beautiful.[94]

---

[92] Lewis, *A Grief Observed*, 49.

[93] Ibid. 73.

[94] Ibid.

Tolkien understood grief as well, having lost both parents by age twelve, as well as enduring the horrors of World War I firsthand, on the battlefront. But it is in his writings where we find him poignantly grappling with death and solace. *The Lord of the Rings*, he stated, "is mainly concerned with Death, and Immortality."[95] In his theory of fairy stories, a genre opposite that of tragedy he notes, a central feature is "the oldest and deepest desire, the Great Escape: the Escape from Death."[96] But whereas tragedy provides an anatomy lesson of catastrophe, fairy story instead provides "the Consolation of the Happy Ending . . . *eucatastrophe*." Fantasy "does not deny the existence of *dyscatastrophe*, of sorrow and failure," these are "necessary to the joy of deliverance;" fantasy does deny "universal final defeat" and serves as *evangelium*, giving a fleeting glimpse of Joy, Joy beyond the walls of the world, poignant as grief."[97]

Thus, Tolkien describes fantasy, like the tale of Middle Earth, as a realm both "wide and deep and

---

[95] JR.R. Tolkien, in a letter of 14th October, 1958.

[96] J.R.R. Tolkien, "On Fairy Stories" in *Tales from the Perilous Realm* (Boston: Harcourt, 2008), 383.

[97] Ibid., 384.

high and filled with many things . . . beauty that is an enchantment, an ever-present peril; both joy and sorrow as sharp as swords."[98]

Thus, in his *Lord of the Rings* Samwise, Frodo, Aragorn and others listen to the song of their journey, "Until their hearts, wounded with sweet words, overflowed, and their joy was like swords, and they passed in thought out to regions where pain and delight flow together and tears are the very wine of blessedness."[99]

As to forgiveness, Lewis and Tolkien both pointed towards Divine forgiveness as the key to our humanity. Lewis stated the problem: "In our own case we accept excuses too easily; in other people's we do not accept them easily enough." But we can only forgive as we are forgiven:

> To excuse what can really produce good excuses is not Christian charity; it is only fairness. To be a Christian means to forgive the inexcusable, because God has forgiven the inexcusable in you.[100]

---

[98] Ibid., 315.

[99] J.R.R. Tolkien, *The Return of the King* (New York: Ballantine, 2001), Book VI.4, 250.

[100] C.S. Lewis, "On Forgiveness" in *The Weight of Glory and Other Addresses* (New York: Collier Books, 1980), 125.

Thus, Lewis's Christ figure in the *Chronicles of Narnia*, Aslan, states of his sacrificial act atoning for Edmund's treachery:

> Though the Witch knew the Deep Magic, there is a magic deeper still that she did not know . . . that when a willing victim who had committed no treachery was killed in a   traitor's stead, the Table would crack and Death itself would start working backward.[101]

Tolkien demonstrated Christ's atonement, empathizing with and ultimately redeeming our broken humanity in striking fashion. Tolkien and Lewis famously disagreed on how to represent figures like Christ in their stories: Lewis's Aslan, son of the Emperor over the Seas and King, a regal Lion (just as Christ was "The Lion of Judah")[102] of Narnia directly represented Christ, whereas Tolkien spread elements of the gospel around in his works.[103] [104] Thus, images of sacrifice and

---

[101] C.S. Lewis, *The Lion, The Witch and the Wardrobe* (New York: Harper, 1994), 178-9.

[102] Genesis 49:9, Hebrews 7:14, Revelations 5:5.

[103] Donald T. Williams, *An Encouraging Thought: The Christian Worldview in the Writings of J.R.R. Tolkien* (Cambridge, Ohio: Christian Publishing House, 2018). Williams book includes the idea that Frodo represents Christ the Priest, Gandalf Christ the Prophet, and Aragorn Christ the King.

forgiveness are rife. Frodo bears in his own body the wounds sustained from carrying the ring to Mount Doom, though it is with Gandalf and Aragorn that we can see forgiveness played out directly. After sacrificing himself to slow the Balrog from catching his friends, Gandalf eventually finds himself under a darkness where "ice fell like rain" and laying on a mountaintop "until my task is done."[105] Gandalf's "task" greatly resembles Christ's atonement:

> I was alone, forgotten, without escape upon the hard horn of the world . . . faint to my ears came the gathered rumour of all lands: the springing and the dying, the song and the weeping. And the slow everlasting groan of overburdened stone.[106]

The parallels to Christ are striking:

Alone, forgotten: "He is despised and rejected by men, a Man of sorrows and acquainted with grief." (Isaiah 53:3)

---

[104] Philip Zaleski and Carol Zaleski, *The Fellowship: The Literary Lives of the Inklings J.R.R. Tolkien, C.S. Lewis, Owen Barfield, Charles Williams* (New York: Farrar, Straus and Giroux, 2015).

[105] J.R.R. Tolkien, *The Two Towers* (New York: Ballantine Books, 2001), 111.

[106] Ibid.

Faint to my ears came the *gathered rumour of all lands*: *the springing and the dying, the song and the weeping:* "Surely He has borne our griefs and carried our sorrows/" (Isaiah 53:4)

And the slow everlasting groan of overburdened stone: "We know that the whole creation groans and travails with labor pains together until now." (Romans 8:22)

It also appears that Tolkien knew his Dante. In his *Inferno*, Dante describes the lower reaches of hell as in fact cold and dark, being far removed from the light and warmth of God's love. There, in a final act of willful defiance, Satan beats his wings to escape only to freeze himself in the lake of hell:

> *The emperor of the reign of misery from*
> *his chest up emerges from the ice . . .*
>
> *Beneath each face extended two huge*
> *wings . . . and those he flapped, and flapped*
>
> *And from his flapping raised three gales*
> *that swept Cocytus, and reduced it all to ice.*[107]

---

[107] Dante, *Inferno* (New York: Modern Library, 2003), translated Anthony Esolen, Canto 34.28-29, 46-52.

Just as Gandalf demonstrates of Christ's work of atonement, so also does Aragorn, the King of Gondor, embody our deliverance:

> "Thus he (Aragorn) became at last the most hardy of living Men, skilled in their crafts and lore, and was yet more than they; for he was elvenwise, and there was a light in his eyes that when they were kindled few could endure. **His face was sad and stern because of the doom that was laid on him, and yet hope dwelt ever in the depths of his heart**, from which mirth would arise at times like a spring from the rock." [108]

Tolkien thus follows Lewis in grounding ultimate forgiveness, and thus our solace, in the person of Christ. As Lewis argued, it is in God that we find the source of meaning and strength:

> God designed the human machine to run on Himself . . . God cannot give us peace and happiness apart from Himself, because it is not there. There is no such thing.[109]

---

[108] Tolkien, *Return of the King*, Appendix A.5, 374.

[109] C.S. Lewis, *Mere Christianity* (New York: Harper Collins, 2001), 50. Book 2 Ch.3 "The Shocking Alternative."

Hamilton admits as much, both our human weakness with "suffering too powerful to name," the need for "forgiveness" and a "grace too powerful to name." Tolkien and Lewis do us the favor of the naming.[110]

Hamilton's Finale: His Story Has Its Eyes on You

Alexander Hamilton's tale ends tragically and ironically (spoiler alert for the American History non-cognizant, a charge to which the author himself confesses) as the principled and courageous Hamilton dies in a duel at the hands of the wavering and cowardly Burr. Their feud had been developing for over a decade, as Burr first switched parties to defeat Hamilton's father-in-law, Philip Schuyler, for a Representative seat in New York in 1791. In 1800, Hamilton opposed Burr and maneuvered in Congress to throw a deadlocked electoral college Jefferson's way in the Presidential Election. Coming in second, Burr became Jefferson's Vice President, but as Jefferson was dropping him from the ticket in the 1804 election, Burr ran for Governor of New York, when Hamilton publicly opposed his candidacy causing Burr to lose.

---

[110] See footnotes 78 - 80.

Hamilton opposed Burr's unprincipled ambition, stating in one letter that Burr would make commitments, "but he will laugh in his sleeve while he makes them and will break them the first moment it may serve his purpose."[111]

The early death of Hamilton, the "ten dollar founding father without a father,"[112] is deeply lamented:

> *Every other founding father's story gets told*
>
> *Every other founding father gets to grow old.[113]*

Hamilton's wife Eliza picks up where Alexander's story trails off. She lives another fifty years on the public front, speaking against slavery and raising funds for the Washington Memorial. In the private, family-oriented sphere, she establishes the first private orphanage in New York City and interviews the soldiers with whom Hamilton fought, seeking to "tell his story."

---

[111] Bernard C. Steiner and James McHenry, *The Life and Correspondence of James McHenry* (Cleveland, OH: Burrows Brothers Co., 1907), 484.

[112] *Hamilton*, I.1.

[113] *Hamilton*, II.23, "Who Lives Who Dies Who Tells Your Story."

Like Alexander, Eliza works "like (she) is running out of time" and wonders if she has done enough, lamenting that had he been around, she could have done so much more. "Will they tell my story?" Eliza wonders. Will the future generations tell Alexander's story? *Hamilton*'s, finale echoes George Washington's farewell address in which he sets out to "teach 'em how to say goodbye."[114] Washington desires, "like the scripture says, . . . (to) sit under my own vine and fig tree, a moment alone in the shade, at home in this nation we've made" yet he anticipates himself "consigned . . . soon to the mansions of rest" having helped establish "good laws under a free government."[115]

To this vision, Lewis counters with his own notion of good, and of Joy. Lewis had no problems with moral crusading, holding that:

> If you read history you will find that the Christians who did most for the present world were precisely those who thought most of the next. It is since Christians have largely ceased to think of the other world that they have become so ineffective in this. Aim at Heaven and

---

[114] *Hamilton*, II.9, "One Last Time."

[115] Ibid.

you will get earth "thrown in": aim at earth and you will get neither[116]

The courage to pursue just such morality itself, while doomed when relying on mere human strength, is thus a gift, a grace "too powerful to mention." But Lewis saw that the matter did not stop simply at the level of the moral:

> God may be more than moral goodness: He is not less. The road to the promised land runs past Sinai. The moral law may exist to be transcended: but there is no transcending it for those who have not first admitted kits claims upon them, and then tried with all their strength to meet that claim, and squarely faced the fact of their failure.[117]

Or as he put it in the finale of his *Space Trilogy*, *That Hideous Strength:*

> Of course there are universal rules to which all goodness must conform. But that's only the grammar of virtue. It's not where the sap is. He doesn't make two

---

[116] Lewis, Mere Christianity, 134.

[117] Lewis, *The Problem of Pain*, 65. Ch. 4 "Human Wickedness."

blades of grass the same: how much less two saints, two nations, two angels.[118]

For Tolkien, the battle between life and death, between good and evil, is the essence of *eucatastrophe*, the "true form of the fairy tale, and its highest function."[119] It implies eventually "the joyous turn" which "does not deny the existence of *dyscatastrophe*, or sorrow and failure: the possibility of these is necessary to the joy of deliverance; it denies universal final defeat and in so far is evangelium, giving a fleeting glimpse of Joy, Joy beyond the walls of the world, poignant as grief."[120]

Thus, like the stories of Alexander Hamilton, his wife Eliza, and even George Washington, Tolkien "en-courages" us that our endings can be like that of the fellowship of Sam, Frodo, Aragorn, and the rest, when the minstrel sings them the song of Frodo the Nine-Fingered and the Ring of Doom,

> Until their hearts, wounded with sweet words, overflowed, and their joy was like swords, and they passed in thought out to

---

[118] Lewis, *That Hideous Strength*, 369.

[119] Tolkien, "On Fairy Stories" in *Tales of the Perilous Realm*, 384.

[120] Ibid.

regions where pain and delight flow together and tears are the very wine of blessedness.[121]

That the phrase "the very wine of blessedness" alludes to the communion cup helps us bring Tolkien and Lewis back home to their source in faith. For all his talk of fairy story and imagination, Tolkien admits "Of course, fairy stories are not the only means of recovery, or prophylactic against loss. Humility is enough."[122] And making the case even more explicit, he states:

> The Gospels contain a fairy story, or a story of a larger kind which embraces the essence of all fairy stories . . . But this story has entered History and the primary world . . . The Birth of Christ is the eucatastrophe of Man's history. The Resurrection is the eucatastrophe of the story of the Incarnation. This story begins and ends in joy.[123]

Martin Luther King drew his source of strength from Scriptural promises as well, alluding to the prophet Amos who delivers God's exhortation:

---

[121] Tolkien, Return of the King, 250

[122] Tolkien, "On Fairy Stories" in *Tales of the Perilous Realm*, 373.

[123] Ibid., "On Fairy Stories: Epilogue," 388.

"Seek me and live . . . But let justice run down like water, and righteousness like a mighty stream."[124]

> Now is the time to make justice a reality for all of God's children . . . No, no, we are not satisfied, and we will not be satisfied until justice rolls down like waters and righteousness like a mighty stream.[125]

Work on America's "Great Unfinished Symphony" goes ever on. Washington's hope to "sit under his own vine and fig tree" (itself an allusion to the prophet Micah, where peace was guaranteed due to the Almighty having spoken)[126] where he could be "at home in the nation we've made"[127] is the proper rest of a life well-lived. Washington's hope for a place in the "mansions of rest" is one best guaranteed by the words of Jesus who promises, "In my Father's house are many mansions."[128] To

---

[124] Amos 5:4, 24.

[125] Martin Luther King, "I Have a Dream," Speech given at the "March on Washington," Copyright 1963. Martin Luther King Jr. Online Available https://www.archives.gov/files/press/exhibits/dream-speech.pdf .

[126] "Everyone will sit under their own vine and under their own fig tree, and no one will make them afraid, for the LORD Almighty has spoken." Micah 4:4.

[127] *Hamilton*, I.9 "One Last Time."

[128] John 14:2.

Alexander's confession, "I'm never satisfied,"[129] Jesus offers that "whoever drinks of the water that I shall give him shall never thirst."[130] To Burr's lament that death "takes [and] History obliterates,"[131] Jesus answers "but the water that I shall give him will become in him a fountain of water springing up into everlasting life."[132] To Burr's refrain that love "takes and it takes and it takes and we keep loving anyway," Scripture reminds us that "we love because He first loved us."[133]

It is perhaps fitting to conclude with Dante's image of Divine Love, depicted in the concluding lines of his *Divine Comedy* as he gazes on Christ:

> *Here ceased the powers of my high fantasy,*
>
> *Already were all my will and my desires*
>
> *Turned – as a wheel in equal balance – by*

---

[129] *Hamilton*, I.11 "Satisfied.."

[130] John 4:14.

[131] Hamilton, II.22 "The World Was Wide Enough."

[132] John 4:14.

[133] 1 John 4:19.

The Love that moves the sun and the other stars.[134]

This love to which *Hamilton* alludes is the love that gives and gives and gives and does not take. It provides the courage and hope to lift all things to eternal significance both in this world and the next. In the face of this love, Hamilton can only stare and state, "You complete me." *Hamilton* is about "America, you Great Unfinished Symphony," of which Hamilton "wrote some notes at the beginning of a song someone will sing for me."[135] But this Unfinished Symphony is in truth a part of Lewis's Great Dance in which the nations are but minute corpuscles amidst the grand and luminous streams of personal beings, all conducted in a Cosmic Orchestra by a Conductor who has fashioned each individual instrument. The sense of a nation finally fades away, as Scripture states, "There is neither Jew nor Gentile, neither slave nor free, there is no male or female, for you are all one in Jesus Christ."[136] And it is an orchestra of

---

[134] Dante, *Paradise*, trans. Anthony Esolen (New York: The Modern Library, 2007), 33:142-145.

[135] *Hamilton*, II.22, "The World Was Wide Enough."

[136] Galatians 3:28.

worship; heaven will be an orchestra in which every nation and tongue sings God's praise to fulfill the vision of the Psalmist: "Let the nations be glad and sing for joy."[137]

In *Hamilton*, the characters exalt in finding themselves in New York City, "the greatest city in the world" where history is "happening," where "the revolution's happening."[138] But it is in what Augustine referred to as the *City of God* where the greatest revolution unfolds, where men turn to God as the source of their love and action. *Hamilton* and its songs saunter, sway, and sigh through the national and earthly travails of a revolution, but such a play only portends what Teilhard de Chardin reminded us of at the beginning, that," the divine assails us, penetrates us, and molds us. We imagined it as distant and inaccessible, whereas in act we live steeped in its burning layers."[139]

---

[137] Psalm 67:4.

[138] *Hamilton*, I.5, "The Schuyler Sisters."

[139] Pierre Teilhard de Chardin, *The Divine Milieu* (1957), quoted in Jeffrey Overstreet, *Through a Screen Darkly*, 5.

RESOURCES

TO CONNECT WITH AN UNEXPECTED JOURNAL

An Unexpected Journal is published quarterly; however, the conversation does not end. Join us on social media for discussion with the authors weekly:

***An Unexpected Journal* online:**
http://anunexpectedjournal.com

On Facebook:
https://www.facebook.com/anunexpectedjournal/

On Twitter: https://twitter.com/anujournal

On Instagram:
https://www.instagram.com/anujournal/

On Pinterest:
https://www.pinterest.com/anunexpectedjournal/

Comments and feedback can be submitted at http://anunexpectedjournal.com/contact/ Be sure to sign up for our newsletter for announcements on new editions and events near you:
http://anunexpectedjournal.com/newsletter

TO READ MORE

When discussing theology, or philosophy, or literature, or art, one is stepping into and taking part of a larger conversation that has been taking place for centuries. Each essay within the journal contains not only the thoughts of the individual author, but draws upon works and thinkers of the past. It is our hope that the writing not only engages your interest in the specific essay topic, but that you join us in the Great Conversation.

To read more, please visit http://anunexpectedjournal.com/resources/ for a list of the works cited within the essays of the journal.

SUBSCRIBE

Yearly subscriptions to *An Unexpected Journal* are available through our web site. Please visit http://anunexpectedjournal.com/subscribe for more information. For bulk pricing, events, or speaking requests, please send an email to anunexpectedjournal@gmail.com.

About An Unexpected Journal

The Inspiration

J. R. R. Tolkien and C. S. Lewis, both members of The Inklings writers group, are well-known for their fiction embedded with Christian themes. These fantasy writers, who were also philosophers and teachers, understood the important role imagination plays in both exercising and expanding the faculties of the mind as well as the development of faith.

Beyond the parables of Jesus, their works are the gold standard for imaginative apologetics. The title, *An Unexpected Journal*, is a nod to the work to which Tolkien devoted much of his life, *The Lord of the Rings*.

Our Story

An Unexpected Journal is the endeavor of a merry band of Houston Baptist University Master of Arts in Apologetics students and alumni. What began as simply a Facebook post on November 1, 2017 wishing that there was an outlet for imaginative apologetics quickly organized by the end of the year into a very real and very exciting quarterly publication.

Our Mission

An Unexpected Journal seeks to demonstrate the truth of Christianity through both reason and the imagination to engage the culture from a Christian worldview.

Our Contributors

Carla Alvarez

Carla Alvarez is a mother to three and a graduate of HBU's Masters in Apologetics program. Her philosophy in both business and apologetics is if what we think affects what we do, then the "how" is just as important as the "what." As actions have a lasting impact, it is of utmost importance to develop right thoughts. She creates effective communications for clients at Legacy Marketing (www.legacymarketingservices.com) and writes about the Christian faith at RaisedtoWalk.org (www.raisedtowalk.org).

Karise Gililland

Karise Gililland is a coach by day, writer by night, 24-hour-a-day mama of two! She holds a BA in English from Southern Methodist University and a Masters in Apologetics from Houston Baptist University.

Lucas W. Holt

Lucas W. Holt is the founder of Pelican Poetry, a literary platform dedicated to perceiving truth through the poetic imagination. He lives and works in Portland, Oregon, where he enjoys hiking, drinking coffee, and exploring the wonders of the Pacific Northwest.

Nicole Howe

Nicole Howe is a wife and homeschooling mother of four and currently resides in Illinois. She is scheduled to graduate with a Masters of Apologetics from Houston Baptist University this fall. When she isn't writing, she enjoys cooking, exploring nature, and performing improv comedy at her local theater.

Jason Monroe

Jason holds a B.A. from York College in York, NE, where he studied English and Psychology. He also recently completed his M.A. in Christian Apologetics from Houston Baptist University. Along with research and writing, Jason plays drums in a band and works in the mental health field. He grew up in Pierre, SD and currently lives in Spearfish, SD. In his spare time, he does a lot of outdoors activities in the Black Hills area and volunteers at his local parish.

Seth Myers

Seth Myers completed his MA in Cultural Apologetics from Houston Baptist University in 2017. As a power systems engineer, he has been involved with transformer diagnostics and rural electrification projects by partnering with NGOs in West Africa. A volunteer with international students through local churches, he enjoys conversations with friends from all cultures. He considers himself rich in friendships across time and space, including but not limited to C.S. Lewis, J.R.R. Tolkien, Bede the Venerable, Augustine, Ravi Zacharias & friends, and many student friends (chess-playing when possible, but not required) typically from throughout Asia. He has recently begun taking online courses in Faulkner University's Doctor of Humanities program.

Annie Nardone

Annie Nardone is a two-year C. S. Lewis Institute Fellow and is currently reading for her Master of Arts in Cultural Apologetics from Houston Baptist University. Her feet are firmly planted in Rohan, Narnia, and Hogwarts, far fairer lands than this. She has researched, photographed, and written a cookbook of historically accurate recipes covering the time between 64 A.D through the Medieval age. Annie resides in Virginia with her fandom-loving family and three sphynx cats who read with her daily but really don't give a tick about her ramblings regarding any of it.

Josiah Peterson

Josiah Peterson is debate coach and instructor of rhetoric at the King's College and is enrolled in HBU's MAA program in Cultural Apologetics. He lives in New York with his wife Rachelle and daughter Hosanna. His primary scholarly interest is in the work of C.S. Lewis.

Daniel Ray

Daniel was the second graduate right behind Zak from the on-line MA in Christian apologetics from Houston Baptist University. He has taught elementary, middle and high school, and is a co-editor of a forthcoming book *The Story of the Cosmos* (Harvest House, August 2019), a collection of essays from astronomers, a theologian or two, astrophysicists, literary scholars and laymen, each sharing their insights about the glory the heavens declare. He is also the cohost of a little podcast called "Good Heavens! A Podcast about the Universe with Wayne and Dan." In his spare time, Daniel runs, reads, writes, stargazes, and bakes apple pie from scratch.

Find Dan's podcast at https://www.patreon.com/GoodHeavens.

Zak Schmoll

Zak Schmoll is the founder of Entering the Public Square (www.enteringthepublicsquare.com), a blog founded on the sincere belief that every Christian should understand the importance of discussing Christianity in the marketplace of ideas. He earned his MA in Apologetics at Houston Baptist University and is currently a PhD student in Humanities at Faulkner University. His work has been featured on several websites including The Federalist, the Public Discourse and the Fourth World Journal.

BIBLIOGRAPHY

Reason for Our Hope

Chesterton, G.K. "The Ethics of Elfland." In *Orthodoxy*. n.d.

Lewis, C.S. *An Experiment in Criticism*. London: Cambridge University Press, 1961.

—. *The Collected Letters of C.S. Lewis*. San Francisco, CA: HarperSanFrancisco, 2004.

MacDonald, George. *The Imagination: Its Function and Its Culture*. n.d.

Tolkien, J.R.R. *On Fairy Stories*. London: HarperCollins, 2014.

Tales of Courage and Hope: Black Panther in Middle Earth and Narnia

Anselm. "Monologion." In *Anselm of Canterbury: The Major Works*, 60-61. Oxford: Oxford University Press, 2008.

Johnston, Robert K. *Reel Spirituality*. Grand Rapids, MI: Baker Academic, 2006.

Lewis, C.S. *Mere Christianity*. New York, NY: HarperOne, 2000.

—. *Screwtape Letters*. New York, NY: HarperCollins, 2000.

—. *The Discarded Image*. Cambridge: Cambridge University Press, 1995.

—. *The Lion, the Witch, and the Wardrobe*. New York, NY: HarperCollins, 1994.

—. "The Gods Return to Earth." *Tim and Tide magazine*, August 14, 1954: 1082.

Markos, Louis. *On the Shoulders of Hobbits: the Road to Virtue with Tolkien and Lewis*. Grand Rapids, MI: Eeardmans, 2012.

Overstreet, Jeffrey. *Through a Screen Darkly*. Ventura, CA: Regal Books, 2007.

Tolkien, J.R.R. "Mythopoeia." 1931.
https://www.poetryfoundation.org/poems/46565/oz
ymandias.

—. *Return of the King.* New York, NY: Ballantine Books, 1994.

—. *The Fellowship of the Ring.* New York, NY: Ballantine Books,
1980.

Hope, Life, and the Fountain of Trevi

La Dolce Vita. Directed by Federico Fellini. Cineriz, 1960.

"History." *The Trevi Fountain.* n.d.
http://www.trevifountain.net/trevifountainhistory3.
htm (accessed September 17, 2015).

Three Coins in a Fountain. Directed by Jean Negulosco. 20th
Century Fox, 1954.

The Lord of the Rings and Consolation Concerning Death

Claason, Tim. "There is No Benign Religion." *Tim Stepping Out.*
May 22, 2015. Accessed June 12, 2018.
https://timsteppingout.wordpress.com/2015/05/22/there
-is-no-benign-religion/.

"Elven Life Cycle." Tolkien Gateway. Accessed October 20,
2016. http://tolkiengateway.net/wiki/Elven_Life_cycle.

Garth, John. *Tolkien and the Great War: The Threshold of
Middle-earth.* New York: Mariner, 2005. iBooks.

Miller, Michael. "C. S. Lewis, Scientism, and the Moral
Imagination," in *The Magician's Twin.* Edited by John
G. West. Seattle: Discovery Institute Press, 2012.

Tolkien, J.R.R. *The Fellowship of the Ring.* New York: Houghton
Mifflin, 1994.

—. *The Letters of J.R.R. Tolkien.* Edited by Humphrey
Carpenter. New York: Houghton Mifflin, 2000.

—. *The Return of the King.* New York: Houghton Mifflin, 1994.

—. *The Two Towers.* New York: Houghton Mifflin, 1994.

—. *On Fairy-stories.* Edited by Verlyn Flieger and Douglas Anderson. London: Harper Collins, 2008.

Lava: A Story of Love and Hope

"5 Questions with Disney/Pixar's LAVA Director James Ford Murphy." *KHON2.* November 3, 2014. http://khon2.com/2014/11/03/5-questions-with-disneypixars-lava-director-james-ford-murphy/. (accessed December 1, 2015).

Davis, Lauren. "The Real Geology Behind Pixar's Short Film Lava." *Io9.* n.d. http://io9.com/the-real-geology-behind-pixars-short-film-lava-1713976956 (accessed December 1, 2015).

Montagne, Renee. "Israel Kamakawiwo'ole: The Voice of Hawaii." *NPR.* April 4, 2011. http://www.npr.org/2010/12/06/131812500/israel-kamakawiwo-ole-the-voice-of-hawaii (accessed December 1, 2015).

The Power in Pain

Lewis, C.S. *A Grief Observed.* New York, NY: HarperCollins, 1996.

Courage in the Cosmos

Austen, Jane. *Pride and Prejudice.* Project Gutenberg, n.d.

Burton, Richard. *The Anatomy of Melancholy.* New York, NY: Review Books, 2011.

Osborne, Hannah. "KIC 8462852: Alien Megastructure Star Starts Dimming Again--What Does It Mean?" *Newsweek.* May 26, 2017. http://www.newsweek.com/kic-8462852-alien-megastructure-dimming-astronomers-baffled-616346/ (accessed March 2, 2018).

Vignale, Giovanni. *The Beautiful Invisible: Creativity, Imagination, and Theoretical Physics.* Oxford: Oxford University Press, 2011.

The Homeric Versus the Christian Ideal of Man

Bulfinch, Thomas. *Mythology.* New York, NY: Random House, 1934.

Homer. *The Odyssey.* Translated by Richard Lattimore. New York, NY: Harper, 2007.

Plato. *Republic.* Translated by Robin Waterfield. New York, NY: Oxford World's Classics, 2008.

Reynolds, John Mark. *When Athens Met Jerusalem.* Downers Grove, IL: IVP Academic, 2009.

The Making of a Hero

Auerbach, Shona. *Dear Frankie.* Miramax, 2004.

Bird, Brad. *The Incredibles 2.* Pixar Animation Studios, 2018.

Brody, Richard. "Review: The Authoritarian Populism of 'Incredibles 2.'" *The New Yorker*, June 19, 2018. Accessed August 30, 2018. https://www.newyorker.com/culture/richard-brody/review-the-authoritarian-populism-of-incredibles-2.

Hattenstone, Simon. "Krzysztof Kieslowski Interviewed for Three Colours Red." *The Guardian*, November 8, 1994. Accessed December 1, 2015. http://www.theguardian.com/film/2011/nov/09/krzysztof-kieslowski-interview.

Howe, Nicole. "Augustine's The Confessions: The Power of Spiritual Autobiography." *An Unexpected Journal* 1, no. 2 (Summer 2018): 65–76. Accessed August 30, 2018. https://anunexpectedjournal.com/augustines-the-confessions-the-power-of-spiritual-autobiography/.

Lewis, C. S. *The Abolition of Man.* New York, NY: HarperCollins, 2001.

Lewis, C.S. "Ajax and Others: John Jones, On Aristotle and Other Greek Tragedy." In *Image and Imagination*, 191–193. New York, NY: Cambridge University Press, 2013.

———. "Our English Syllabus." In *Image and Imagination*, edited by Walter Hooper, 21–33. New York, NY: Cambridge University Press, 2013.

———. "The Four Loves." In *The Family Christian Library: The Beloved Works of C.S. Lewis*, 211–288. Grand Rapids, MI: Family Christian Press, 1960.

———. *Till We Have Faces: A Myth Retold*. New York, NY: Harcourt, Inc., 1956.

Markos, Louis. *Restoring Beauty: The Good, The True, and The Beautiful in the Writings of C.S. Lewis*. Colorado Springs, CO: Biblica Publishing, 2010.

"Shona Auerbach." *ShonaAuerbach.Com*, n.d. Accessed December 1, 2015. http://www.shonaauerbach.com/.

Tales of Courage and Hope: Hamilton in Middle Earth and Narnia

Brantley, Ben. "Young Rebels Changing History and Theater." *New York Times*. August 6, 2015. https://www.nytimes.com/2015/08/07/theater/review-hamilton-young-rebels-changing-history-and-theater.html (accessed August 15, 2018).

Dante. *Inferno*. New York, NY: Modern Library, 2003.

—. *Paradise*. Translated by Anthony Esolen. New York, NY: The Modern Library, 2007.

Lewis, C.S. *A Grief Observed*. New York, NY: Bantam, 1976.

—. *Christian Reflections*. Grand Rapids, MI: Eerdmans, 1975.

—. *Mere Christianity*. San Francisco, CA: HarperSanFrancisco, 2001.

—. *Miracles*. New York, NY: Collier, 1978.

—. *Perelandra*. New York: Scribner, 2003.

—. *Screwtape Letters*. New York, NY: HarperCollins, 2000.

—. *Surprised by Joy*. Glasgow: Colins, 1955.

—. *That Hideous Strength*. New York: Scribner, 2003.

—. *The Four Loves*. New York, NY: Harcourt, 1991.

—. *The Great Divorce*. New York, NY: HarperOne, 2000.

—. *The Lion, the Witch, and the Wardrobe.* New York, NY: HarperCollins, 1994.

—. *The Magician's Nephew.* Norwalk, CT: Easton Press, 1983.

—. *The Weight of Glory and Other Essays.* New York: Collier Books, 1980.

—. *Till We Have Faces.* New York, NY: Harcourt, 1985.

Markos, Louis. *The Life and Writings of C.S. Lewis.* The Great Courses. Chantilly, VA: The Teaching Company, 2000.

Miranda, Lin-Manuel. "Hamilton." *Hamilton.* 2015.

Overstreet, Jeffrey. *Through a Screen Darkly.* Ventura, CA: Regal Books, 2007.

Steiner, Bernard C., and James McHenry. *The Life and Correspondence of James McHenry.* Cleveland, OH: Burrows Brothers Co., 1907.

Thompson, Francis. "The Hound of Heaven." In *Oxford Book of English Mystical Verse.* 1917.

Tolkien, J.R.R. "Mythopoeia." 1931. https://www.poetryfoundation.org/poems/46565/ozymandias.

—. *Tales from the Perilous Realm.* Boston, MA: Harcourt, 2008.

—. *The Hobbit.* New York, NY: Ballantine Books, 1986.

—. *The Monters and the Critics and Other Essays.* London: HarperCollins, 2006.

—. *The Return of the King.* New York, NY: Ballantine, 2001.

—. *The Two Towers.* New York, NY: Ballantine Books, 2001.

Williams, Donald T. *An Encouraging Thought: The Christian Worldview in the Writings of J.R.R. Tolkien.* Cambridge: Christian Publishing House, 2018.

Zaleski, Philip, and Carol Zaleski. *The Fellowship: The Literary Lives of the Inklings J.R.R. Tolkien, C.S. Lewis, Owen Barfield, Charles Williams.* New York, NY: Farrar, Straus and Giroux, 2015.

THOUGHTS FROM A FELLOW TRAVELER

By Jack Tollers

If you aren't a Christian and have somehow gotten to the point where you are reading this, then I must warn you about the pebble in your shoe. For that is what it is like to be around Christians who discuss things together, whether or not they are "Christian kinds of things" that are discussed. At a certain point you will notice something about their point of view, something in their underlying assumptions, and to be honest when you do it will become quite annoying.

That is the pebble I was referring to.

But it gets worse.

Maybe it is not your fault that you happen to be reading this, and you've done a pretty good job milling about life without bumping into too much of this sort of Christian stuff. It could be the case that you haven't really made a conscious effort to avoid Christianity, but chances are (if you are reading this) that is going to change. Somewhere along the line, perhaps even in the course of reading this journal, even, a pebble has worked its way into your shoe, and eventually the pebble will have to be dealt with.

It's not my job to tell you what it is. (I don't really know what "it" is in your case. All I know is that when the pebble got into my shoe, it got to the point where I couldn't walk much further without annoying my heel something terrible.) What I can do is suggest to you something that would have helped me if I had come across it in the back of some obscure academic journal: The pebble does not exist for itself. The pebble makes you stop and deal with the pebble. Stopping to deal with the pebble leads to thinking about your shoe. Then you start thinking about how much further up the trail you'd be if it weren't for that blasted pebble, which leads to thoughts about the trail itself and the path you're walking . . . and so on.

A particular Christian, or a particular thought expressed by a Christian, or perhaps just the particular quality you meet in places and things of

Christian origin will eventually function to put you in mind of something beyond or behind themselves. I say something because I'm trying to be non-partisan, but really I mean someone. Because at some point, the context for these thoughts will change to an awareness that this Christ person has been behind all of it.

When this moment comes, avoid mistaking Jesus for the pebble in your shoe. (If you do, it won't be long before another pebble gets in there and starts the whole thing off again. It took me years to figure that out.) Instead, consider the possibility that he is more like the path than the pebble. He said as much himself when he told Thomas, "I am the way, the truth and the life. No man comes to the Father except by me."

The truth aspect of Jesus's claim is, of course, exclusive. But there is more to his self-disclosure. The other terms, "the way" and "the life" point us beyond a mere static assertion of fact or a single point of view toward a dynamic process of relational involvement. The pursuit of truth leads to knowing Jesus (if he indeed is truth incarnate). Thus, just as travelers come to know a country by living in it and exploring it, so people will grow in their knowledge of Truth as they make their way through life, the path itself bringing us in proximity to Jesus.

Such a journey, so conceived, is bound to take a person through some interesting experiences, and to unexpected places. Once the pebble is out of the shoe.

> All the way to heaven is heaven for he said, "I am the way" — St. Catherine of Sienna

> "And ye shall seek me, and find me, when ye shall search for me with all your heart." — Jeremiah 29:13

Made in the USA
Columbia, SC
24 December 2019